Guide

Westphalian Open Air Museum
Detmold

D0595300

Published by order of
Landschaftsverband Westfalen-Lippe
(Regional Federation of Westphalia Lippe)

Westphalian Open Air Museum Detmold
by Stefan Baumeier

Stefan Baumeier
G. Ulrich Großmann
Wolf-Dieter Könenkamp

Guide

Westphalian
Open Air Museum
Detmold
Museum of Rural History
and Culture

© by Landschaftsverband Westfalen-Lippe
(Regional Federation of Westphalia Lippe)
Westphalian Open Air Museum Detmold 1989

Editors: Stefan Baumeier and Kurt Dröge

Design: Horst Wasgindt

English translation: D. and Chr. Zeuner and Lore Schäfer

Production: Küster-Pressedruck · 4800 Bielefeld 11

ISBN 3-926160-05-5

Foreword

The idea of bringing together various types of agricultural buildings in an open air museum is approximately 100 years old. The first open air museums appeared in Scandinavia and were born of a desire to preserve the relics of a rural heritage and to investigate the rural way of life in the past centuries. Thus, as long ago as the end of the 19th century, agricultural life was recognised as having had a crucial part to play in shaping our cultural traditions. However, unlike their counterparts in the art world, the monuments to our rural heritage are still struggling to gain acceptance as evidence of the often harsh and wretched conditions endured by our forefathers. And this process has not been assisted by the transformation of household effects, furniture and other artefacts into items of nostalgia to be displayed as antiques in modern homes. Farmhouses and cottages used as weekend retreats provide us with few clues as to their actual history.

Open air museums, therefore, have a vital role to play in preserving selected items of rural culture so that both we and future generations can gain an insight into the kind of world which our ancestors inhabited. In the protective and controlled environment of such an open air museum and based on a proper scientific and educational concept, these monuments can tell us much about the lives, needs and working conditions of their former occupants.

The Westphalian Open Air Museum at Detmold has set itself the taks of assembling a representative selection of historically important rural buildings, agricultural and otherwise, from all over Westphalia and Lippe. It is thus hoped that visitors, and in particular the young, will begin to see history as a process involving the lives of ordinary people, their work, their ideas and their suffering and not merely as a series of power games played by the rich and the mighty. At a time when the face of the countryside is being transformed at an ever-increasing rate, this aspect of the work of the Landschaftsverband Westfalen-Lippe in preserving our cultural heritage has assumed particular importance.

The idea of establishing an Open Air Museum of Rural History and Culture in Westphalia is not a new one. As long ago as 1954 resources were made available for this purpose — albeit on a fairly modest scale at first — by the Landschaftsverband Westfalen-Lippe. When work was eventually begun in Detmold in 1966 almost all of the buildings which were intended for re-erection had already been acquired. Those which are not yet accessible to the public are still in the process of being re-built or restored. By 1981 it had been possible to re-erect as many as 70 buildings, leaving a further 100 still to be completed. As well as being the first of several village complexes to be partially re-established, the Paderborn Village also houses the first areas to be set aside in the Museum for exhibitions on a variety of subjects.

Although the Westphalian Open Air Museum at Detmold is still developing, there is already a wealth of interesting things for the visitor to see. Together with a selection of more specialised literature on a number of the exhibits and educational packs designed for use in the classroom, this guide should enable children and adults alike to enjoy a meaningful and memorable visit to this museum. Books can never convey the unique impression left on the visitor on his walk through the museum with its ever growing variety.

Detmold, 1982   Josef Sudbrock
                                                 — Landesrat —

The rapidly progressing building activities in the Westphalian Open Air Museum called for supplements to the guidebook. Meanwhile more than a dozen historical buildings have been added, chiefy in the Paderborn village which already features a closed settlement comprising a great variety of different types of buildings and social groups. The next village will shortly be open to the pubic covering buildings from the Sauerland. In the new addition, some mistakes have been corrected which had slipped into the first, but on the whole, the descriptions have been left as they were. New findings of research have, of course, been included, such as new dates referring to the individual buildings. May this edition be as successful as the first.

Detmold, 1989   Friedhelm Nolte
— Landesrat —

The Westphalian Open Air Museum of Rural History and Culture, Detmold

The decision taken by the Regional Committee of the Landschaftsverband Westfalen-Lippe in 1960 to build the Westphalian Open Air Museum of Rural History and Culture in Detmold provided the basis for the realisation of a long-cherished dream.

Approximately 80 hectares of land was set aside for this purpose by the Landesverband Lippe, and now, against the backcloth of the beautiful and historic Teutoburger Wald, one of the largest open air museums in Europe is gradually being assembled. Work began in 1966 under the direction of Prof. Dr. Josef Schepers, who led the operation until 1976. He not only formulated a comprehensive programme of action, but also set about recovering and salvaging dozens of historically important buildings and collecting an impressive array of traditional artefacts from all over the region. When it first opened in 1971 the Museum consisted of the groups of buildings which comprise the moated farm from the Münsterland, the farms from Minden and Osnabrück and two day-labourers' cottages. In 1981, the first phase of the Paderborn Village was opened to the public. Work continued in line with the original plan, and to date 90 buildings have been re-erected in the various settlement groups.

Between 1977 and 1980, in parallel with the reconstruction of the various traditional buildings, a programme of infrastructural work was initiated. In addition to supplying the Museum with water, electricity and gas and installing a security system, a self-contained water course with deep wells, pumps and gravity tanks was built to supply the streams and ponds. This water course will also power the planned watermills.

The construction unit which was established in 1975 contains among other things the workshops where the timber-framed buildings, furniture and implements of various kinds are restored.

The primary task of this Open Air Museum is to investigate,

record and document the rural history and culture of Westphalia. The various combinations of buildings, surrounded as they would have been in their natural state by gardens, fields, meadows, or arable land, are arranged in units which reflect the diversity of settlement patterns, building techniques, lifestyles and economic conditions which once characterised the landscape of Westphalia.

Different types of buildings from every corner of rural Westphalia are or will eventually be featured: thus, for example, the Münsterland and the western part of the Ruhrgebiet are represented by the predominant form of settlement in those regions, namely the isolated farmstead; Minden, Ravensberg, Lippe and Osnabrück by a cluster of farms: the Paderborn region by a village of arable farmsteads and artisans' houses surrounding a church in the centre and a fortified church yard, the Sauerland by a small village; and the Siegen and Wittgenstein areas by a hamlet. Chapels and wayside shrines, windmills and watermills complete this complex and fascinating pattern of human settlement.

20th century houses and their fixtures and fittings are as much at home here as structures from the 15th century — the oldest in the Museum. However, no attempt has been made to reconstruct buildings discovered on archeological sites.

Differences between the social classes are highlighted by the examples of large and small farms, tenanted cottages, the houses of retired farmers and artisans, and those occupied by the landed gentry, farm labourers and villagers.

From a historical point of view, the construction techniques exemplified by the North German hall-house in its various forms and with its diverse arrangement of rooms contrast sharply with those employed in building the type of house commonly found in the Siegerland region of central Germany. Different building materials, uses of colour and forms of decoration are as unique as the different parts of Westphalia from which they come.

Some buildings have not been altered in any way since the time they were built, whilst others display the tell-tale signs of renovation or modification. Although household furnishings and effects have been authentically arranged in their traditional contexts so as to demonstrate their original purpose, the mode of presentation adopted — which is obviously constrained both by the limits of our knowledge and by the scope of the Museum — should not be literally interpreted as reflecting the realities of life in the past. The Open Air Museum can only hope to give a partial and approximate account of historical truth.

The Museum is also engaged in assembling specialised collections of items representing the historical and cultural heritage of Westphalia. A new main entrance is planned for the north-east tip of the site, together with a communications centre, seminar rooms, a vehicle park and a main restaurant. This complex will also include a purpose-built exhibition hall to house the comprehensive collection of historical artefacts which at present fall into the following main categories: folk art, household effects, childrens' toys, pewterware, ceramics, traditional costume and dress, textile-making, jewellery, trade and transport, weights and measures, forms of wall decoration, agricultural machinery, the history of education and architectural remains.

In the meantime, the visitor can see at least a small part of this rich and impressive collection in the temporary exhibition area which has been established in the barn from Westendorf in the Paderborn Village. The Museum also carries out research in areas such as the design, construction and use of buildings, the history of handicrafts and other artefacts and the social and cultural traditions of Westphalia. It maintains an archive of photographs and prints, as well as a library containing books on a variety of specialist subjects.

The Open Air Museum sets out to give the visitor a meaningful and rewarding insight into an important part of Germany's rural past. A more commercialised approach would undoubtedly detract from this primary objective and is therefore out of the question. However, to provide a better understanding of the various facets of the working life of a traditional rural community, a number of different work processes are vividly demonstrated; for example, two millers are employed to operate the three wind- and watermills. The ancient methods of historical craftsmanship are shown day by day in the pottery and smithy. Trades which were supplementary to the farm work such as spinning and weaving are demonstrated in their respective rural environments. Following the seasons, the visitors are also made familiar with the gardening and can see the farmers working in the fields.

A The Paderborn village

The Paderborn Village comprises the largest single complex of buildings — 70 altogether — in the Open Air Museum at Detmold. The numerous houses and outbuildings, often huddled in tight clusters, are grouped around the central church with its walled cemetery and the village green with its pond. The entire complex is separated from the surrounding cornfields by a garden. Its layout is modelled on villages in the district of Höxter, and many of its buildings come from the area around the former bishopric of Paderborn which included the imperial abbey at Corvey and the surrounding countryside, and which today encompasses the districts of Paderborn and Höxter als well as parts of Gütersloh, Lippe, Soest and Hameln-Pyrmont. Höxter was characterised by very compact, densely populated villages, in stark contrast to the scattered settlements which typify Westphalia. The village in the Museum looks very much as it would have done at the turn of the last century: 16th century houses stand shoulder to shoulder with those of the 19th century; many of them have undergone numerous alterations or have been extended in some way.

The different social origins of the various buildings reflect the diverse yet closely interconnected social structure of the village. They include the living and working accommodation of farmers and craftsmen, day-labourers and workers, traders and retired farmers, and of the priest and the prince's senior administrator. Communal buildings such as the church, the school and the fire station complete the picture.

The oldest buildings which come from villages along the upper reaches of the Weser date from as far back as the early 16th century. Each farm consists of a handful of buildings; granaries, which were still commonplace in the 17th century, are the exception rather than the rule. More often than not, the only outbuildings were a barn, an implement shed or a cow-house. Some of the houses from the 16th century have hinghly ornate gables which are brightly painted and display elaborate carvings and decorative inscriptions. The jettied gables rest on dragon beams rather than on the more old-fashioned braces or brackets.

The village street. The building to the right is the smithy

Brick-nogging is a much favoured feature of 18th century facades, whereas most of the half timbered houses of the 17th century (Thirty Years War) and those of the 19th century are much more modest in appearance. From the 18th century onwards thatched roofs gradually gave way to tiles and sandstone slates from the Solling mountains.

The oldest farmhouses in the village are half-timbered buildings with high walls and threshing floors at their centre or in one of the side-aisles. In the middle of the 16th century these threshing floors became through passages stretching from one gable wall to the other and were flanked on either side by aisles which contained the living quarters. The parlour was situated at the front of the building and looked out on to the street; a number of the houses have had projecting bays added specifically to extend the parlour, so as to allow a better view of the street. By 1500, the "anchor beam" method of construction had already been superseded by the more modern "post-and-tie-beam" method of timber-framing.

A 5 Churchyard granary

from the Meierhof farm
Borchen-Etteln, district of Paderborn
built in 1576
dismantled in 1976, re-erected in 1984 – 85

In Etteln, the renaissance granary of the Meierhof farm was not included in the churchyard fortification, but stood on a long wall above the valley of the river Alme. Since 1381, the farm of the upper village has been mentioned under various designations. The farmstead which was part of the land owned by the monastery in Böddeken may well be dating further back. In the late middle ages, this was the official farm of the monastery in Etteln wich owned considerable real estate in the area. A sheepfold comprising a maximum of 500 sheep was leased together with the farm ever since the early years of the fifteenth century, after the place had been deserted for some time. A granary served to store the payments made in kind by the surrounding monasterial leaseholds. In 1530, the "Spieker" has been recorded as having been inhabited from time to time. The last occupants of the granary which has now been re-erected in the museum were Polish workers who lived in it during World War II.

The granary covers a ground surface of approximately 6 x 11 meters on a slightly sunk-in high quarry stone base. The timbered part made of exceptionally thick wood shows wall braces from the sill to the frame posts, a type of bracing which otherwise occurred in Westphalia as late as in the 19th century. The gable pediments are jettied on tie beams. The filling structures are decorated with simple ornamental patterns carved by the carpenters. In the open air museum, the granary was erected as it would have looked at the turn of the century (1900). The obvious signs of coaking on the front gable are somewhat younger, witnessing a fire in an outbuilding of the farm in Etteln. Various changes inside the building tell that the granary must have been used as a dwelling place from time to time. In this connection, a suspended lavatory had been attached to the left eaves wall but was removed again in the 19th century. Early in our century, a baking vault was attached to the rear gable wall for some time. In Etteln, the building had to make way for the straightening of a river.

Granary on its original site   *1976*

Churchyard granary in the Paderborn village

A 6 Churchyard granary

von Wrede,
Anröchte-Mellrich, in the district of Soest,
built in 1505,
dismantled in 1969 and re-erected in 1981 – 82

In the late Middle Ages, granary-like structures were sometimes erected at the edge of fortified churchyards in order to give better protection to that most precious of buildings, the village church. Often, several such buildings would be positioned at various points around the church to form a defensive barrier. In more recent times buildings such as these or their successors were used for storage purposes or as sheds, and some were even converted into workshops or small houses.

The example from Mellrich is a two-storey timber-framed building with a high cellar on ground level. The coating of clay on the outer walls, with only the studs in the eaves walls still visible, is a typical feature of buildings from the Middle Ages. The clay facing conceals a timber frame with large panels which are reinforced with intersecting diagonal braces; the slender

The Mellrich churchyard granary being re-erected

laths of oak to which the clay has been applied are secured to these braces and to the horizontal rails with nails. The roof, which overhangs to an exceptional degree on all four sides, is supported on a series of wooden brackets. Towards the end of the 18th century it was partly destroyed by fire and was restored, along with the rear gable, around 1790. In keeping with the style of the day, arch braces were inserted in the new gable wall, which was then infilled with brick-nogging; its clay coating was not replaced. The hatch in the front gable was added around the same time.

A 9 – 12 The Valepage farm

This group of buildings represents what would have been a large and economically important farm possessing somewhere in the region of 40 hectares of land. They occupy a prominent position opposite the main entrance to the churchyard and consist of a farmhouse which came from the Valepage farm in Delbrück, a barn situated directly alongside and parallel to it, and a granary.

In the space between these three buildings stands a horse-engine of the late 19th century which once powered an animal-feed chopper or a threshing machine on the threshing floor of the farmhouse (A 9). The engine or "gin" was turned by horses treading a circular path around it paved for this particular purpose. The garden, which is situated on a raised terrace, is reached by a covered stairway whose gate posts are decorated with ornamental flowers and bear the date of construction *(ANNO 1760)*. Adjoining the garden is a small orchard which contains a fruit-drying kiln.

The Valepage farm. The granary comes from Winkhausen and the barn from Westendorf

A 9 Farmhouse

from the Valepage farm in Delbrück-Dorfbauerschaft
in the district of Paderborn, built in 1577,
partly reconstructed in the 19th century,
dismantled in 1973 and re-erected in 1975 – 79

The Valepage farm was undoubtedly the most important in the
Delbrück region and is famous for its richly carved Renaissance facade.

The farm is first mentioned in the records compiled by the monastery at Abdinghof between 1337 and 1355 where it is referred to as Lake farm. The entry
for 1385 names a certain *"Walter vame Wygmodeberge geheten Valepage"* a
man of noble birth. Sometime prior to 1481 a member of the aristocratic von
Varendorff family which had its own seal and coat of arms, married into the
Valepage family. The farm formed part of the estate owned by the Abdinghof
monastery and was leased to the Valepage-Varendorff family, which of course
also had land of its own. Indeed, apart from the Bishop of Paderborn, they
were the only resident landowners in the Delbrück region. In 1649 the farm is
known to have had a total of 40 hectares of land, half pasture and half arable;
according to an inventory drawn up at the time, by 1679 only 16 hectares remained. Several of the outlying tenanted farms were dependent on the Valepage farm for their very existence, as was the day-labourer whose cottage
("Haußstette") was attached to the farm itself. Despite its size, it occasionally
ran into debt, particularly at the beginning of the 17th century. Numerous members
of the Valepage family held public office, including, for a time, the post of chief
judicial officer of the district (in the service of the Bishop of Paderborn) and that
of clerk to the provincial court, an important administrative office, for the privi-
lege of which Johan D. Valepage was prepared to pay 180 taler. As a result of
being invested with these offices, the family is reputed to have moved to
Delbrück in the 18th century. Following the death of the last surviving member
of the family in 1845, the farm was exclusively leased to tenants, and an inventory from that time records it has having 50 hectares of land, although only 16
ha were available to the tenant.

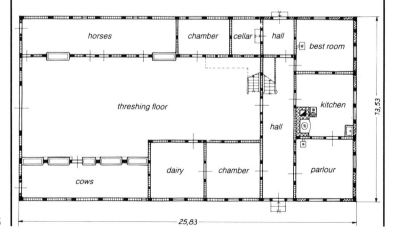

Valepage farm — inscription above the entrance to the threshing floor

This magnificent aisled house, a four post and beam structure which was attached to the Valepage farmhouse, was built in 1557, as the inscription above the entrance to the threshing floor confirms:

Dis Haus steit in Gots hant. Joist Valpage ist er gnant
Der hats lassen bawen Und auf Got gesetz sein vertrawe
Anno Domini   1577.

In the Museum it has been restored to look very much as it would have done at the turn of the last century when it was tenanted property. The front gable, which dates from 1577, has survived almost completely intact. Thanks to its elegant Renaissance carvings, this highly decorative facade is one of the most beautiful to be found anywhere in North Germany. The infill panels above each of the sills are sealed with wood in order to provide a larger surface area for the carved ornamentation. Here the studs and panels are overlaid with a frieze of half-rosettes, whilst the intervening spandrels display representations of things as diverse as dragons and the Resurrection of Christ. The uniformity of decoration is interrupted at one point to depict a pack of hounds chasing a hare. Even the sills are adorned with images of fabulous creatures and scenes from the Bible (e.g. a stag by a well, symbolising baptism), as well as the busts of a man and a woman (probably the original owners). The significance of the initials
AISD. HB. D. B. ASG. HMS. embossed on one of the panels is not yet clear.
The inscription above the door is flanked by two coats of arms which were painted on in the 20th century and attest to the aristocratic origins of the von Hülst (on the left) or Valepage families.
It is obvious from the outer face of the right-hand wall that the house has been substantially altered on two separate occasions. The rear section of the aisle on the right was reconstructed at the beginning of the 19th century, and around 1880 the original suite of chambers and the "kitchen" were completely demolished and replaced with a two-storey living

area, the thin timber frame of which was infilled with brick. Originally, the stalls in the two side-aisles at the upper end of the building were not partitioned off from the threshing floor. In the 19th century the timbers in front of the stables were sealed and the lower end of the left-hand aisle was sectioned off to provide accommodation for the maid servants below and the farm hands up above. A dairy and a living room were subsequently added at the far end of the cattle stalls in the aisle on the right. A channel which houses the drive-shaft from the horse-engine runs across the left-hand aisle and through to the threshing floor.

A double door leads into the two-storey living area, which was constructed towards the end of the 19th century. A cross-passage, reminiscent in some ways of the type of kitchen-cum-living area found in older houses, provides access to the rooms on both floors. At ground level, the floor of the cross-passage is composed of flagstones which were produced in Mettlach sometimes between 1880 and 1885. The walls are lined with stencil paintings of a type much favoured in the 19th century. The three rooms on the ground floor comprise a parlour which contains a Warstein stove; a kitchen with a large cooking range (notice the pot in the wall which was used for heating the animal feed); and on the far left, a "best room", whose period furniture gives it an air of austere splendour. The upper storey contains a children's bedroom (on the right), a smoke-bay (also used as a store-room) and finally the master bedroom.

The "best room" in the Valepage house

A 10 Multi-purpose barn

from the Gössman/Severing farm
in Warstein-Westendorf in the district of Soest,
built in 1763,
dismantled in 1967 and re-erected in 1977 – 79

This barn, which is 26.23 metres long, is divided into three sections: a sheep fold beyond the portal in the front gable, an adjoining transverse threshing floor, which is entered through a low door in the right-hand side wall, and a stable at the rear, which is easily recognised from the outside by the open-fronted portico where the horses were unharnessed. Each wall of this timber-framed building is lined with three rows of horizontal rails and reinforced with arch braces. The weatherboarded gable pediment is jettied and supported by dragon beams. Planks of wood were used to infill the lower panels of the walls which enclose the sheepfold; however, those in the eaves walls, along with other parts of the structure which had begun to decay, were replaced in the 19th century by quarry-stone walling. The remains of an inscription can be seen on the lintel above the door which leads on to the threshing floor:

WER AUF GOT TRAUET   DERR HAT WOL
GEBAUET MISTGVNST / DER MENSCHEN SCHADET
MIR NICHT   WAN MIR GOT DEN SEGEN GIEBTT /
ANTON GOSSMANN VND ANNA MARIA   ...HOFF
EHELEUTE HABEN DIESES /
GEBE .... N.HA./M F / JHS

The rear section of the building is divided into two storeys. On the ground floor are the stables which contain a well. The portico in front of the stables is something one would not normally expect to see in Westphalia. The space above the stables might well have served as accommodation for the farm hands

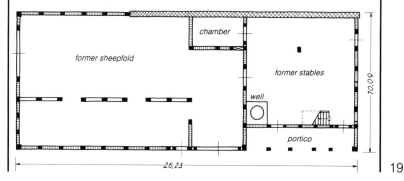

and as a store for animal feed. The huge attic, which spans the entire length and breadth of the building, was used for storing straw and hay. In the Museum this barn is presently being used as a temporary exhibition area where the visiting public can see at least part of the large collection of historical artefacts.

A 11 Granary

from the Wilper farm in Salzkotten-Winkhausen
in the district of Paderborn,
built in 1561,
dismantled in 1973 and re-erected in 1975

A few examples of 16th century granaries inlaid with carved rosettes can still be found in the countryside around Paderborn. Unusually, however, the granary from Wilper is not endowed with the rectangular breast panels normally associated with these buildings, but is adorned instead with half-rosettes inserted between the studs in the gable pediment. A unique feature for this region are the small rafters in the upper gable, which project beyond the sill of the jetty and have spherical ends.

Like its fortified counterpart on the moated farm, this granary also has an external staircase leading to the upper storey — the mark of a very old building indeed. Here, the steps are shielded from the rain by a catslide roof. The door which leads into the upper storey is the original one.

The granary with its frieze of rosettes and distinctive rafters

There are no dividing walls inside the building, and at ground level the structure is supported only by an octagonal column at its centre.

A 12 Fruit-drying kiln

from the Falkenflucht farm
in Höxter-Falkenflucht in the district of Höxter,
built in the 19th century,
dismantled and re-erected in 1980

This quarry stone kiln originally stood in the orchard on the Falkenflucht farm near Bödexen. It was used until 1952 for drying plums, apples and pears which were laid on wattlework hurdles and pushed through the large mouth at the front on to the wooden rack inside. During the fruit crop the kiln was operated day and night. When drying, the fruit was turned at regular intervals, as this shortened the process considerably. The firing chamber is situated at the rear of the kiln, and from here the smoke was guided through a system of pipes situated under the floor and in the walls, thus ensuring that the heat was evenly applied to the fruit. Fruit could only be kept in large quantites if it had been dried, and this process therefore played an important part in the cycle of rural self-sufficiency. However, purpose-built kilns were comparatively rare, and baking ovens were normally used for drying fruit.

Front view of the fruit-drying kiln from Falkenflucht

A 13 Tenanted farmhouse/Dower house

from Heinrich Lindhorst farm
of Lügde-Rischenau, district of Lippe,
built in 1732, reconstructed in 1830,
dismantled in 1968, re-erected in 1986—87

Wilhelm Schröder, the tenant of the small cottage on lot 20 in Rischenau had the dower house erected in 1732, and lived in it with his wife after he had handed the farm to his son Dietrich Adolph in 1755. For his own subsistence he kept "1 acre of farmland, the field at the Scharpenberg and one third of the meadow" in addition to the dower house. When the builder of the dower house had died in 1764, the building was first let to a family. The dower house kept changing its occupants until it was dismantled in 1968, i.e. retired farmers alternated with tenants for approximatel 200 years. Whenever there was no re-tired farmer to live in it, the house was let to day labourers, migrating workers or small craftsmen. The last retired farmer's wife, Dorothee Sophie Lindhorst died on April 5, 1900. Two subsequent families lived in the small outbilding as tenants until 1968.

The small farm of the "small cottage tenant" Schröder (renamed Lindhorst in 1833 by his son-in-law) covered approximately 20 acres of land ever since the 17th century, whereas the tenants of the dower house never had any land of their own, and for this reason never owned any agricultural implements, wagons, or carts. In the stalls they normally kept two cattle or a few goats. The Uhe family moved into the house at the turn of the century. They had several children and were not only short of living space, but had serious problems gaining their livelihood. After the death of her husband who had been working in a brickyard, Mrs. Uhe was left to keep up her large family alone.

Painting of the farm and dower house   *about 1960*
Lindhorst in Rischenau

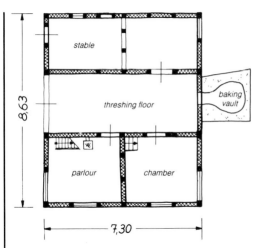

The dower house of the Heinrich Lindhorst farm from Rischenau (no. 20) is one of the rare types of a North German hall house: It is a three post and beam structure. Measuring 7.30 m in total length, it is wider than deep, i.e. 8.63 meters wide. The inscription on the arch above the door tells the year of construction

Anno 1732

At the time, the building was four bays deep. A reconstruction early in the 19th century mostly affected the walls at the right hand side of the house which were partly renewed and changed by additional partitions. The narrow threshing floor reaching right through to the rear gable is located in the centre. The right hand aisle accommodates the parlour next to the front gable and an adjoining chamber on the ground floor, as well as a long chamber on top of the two rooms. These rooms are the only ones in the house lit by one or two windows, respectively. The left hand aisle with its deeply projecting roof at the low off-side accommodates stalls or stables and storage space on top. A baking vault is attached to the rear gable wall, operated from the threshing floor where no daylight is provided.

The condition of the house as it stands in the museum is that of the years immediately following the turn of the last century and shows that neither a chimney nor a water pump were available in the house. The open fireplace — used for cooking — was inside te threshing floor and the smoke of it darkened the walls of the threshing floor in a way which made people abstain from any painting for decades. The house was funished with the mere necessities, new equipment could not be acquired. The attached baking vault was used by the occupants of the dower house and the main farm house, as well as by the surrounding neighbours.

A 14 – 16 Large farm

This farmstead is a reconstruction of farm No. 2 (Wilhelm Zeddies) from the village of Grohnde. It consists of a house, a barn which lies directly alongside and parallel to it and a shed (planned), which marks the edge of the farmyard towards the foot of the slope. The front gable looks out onto the street and is separated from it by a wall and a double iron gate.

The red sandstone which comes from the Weser basin is employed throughout the farm for walls, steps and floors; a particular feature of the Weser region is the use of this material as a covering for roofs.

A 14 Farmhouse

from the Wilhelm Zeddies Farm,
in Emmerthal-Grohnde
in the district of Hameln-Pyrmont,
built in 1731,
dismantled in 1970 and re-erected in 1979 – 81

This farmhouse has a transverse threshing floor – a very modern phenomenon indeed for the early 18th century – which was confined to the rear of the building and was thus no longer entered by vehicles through the front gable, but through a large door in the eaves wall. The living quarters are situated at either side of the corridor, which also represents a significant departure from the traditional layout of houses in this region. A particularly characteristic feature of the building is the decorative facade with its frieze of symmetrical angle braces and its herring-bone brickwork. The external stone steps, the front door and the windows, with which the ground floor is generously endowed, are all designed to draw attention to this house, oriented as it is towards the street. It is also interesting to note that pine as well as oak was used in its construction.

Johann Wilhelm Zeddies acquired farm No. 2 in Grohnde around 1725 and almost immediately began building a new house, which took until 1731 to complete. Frequent reference is made to this house in 18th century documents, and according to an inventory published in 1775 it had 21.5 hectares of arable land and 1.5 hectares of grazing land. During this period the house was occupied by the Zeddies family (there were five children altogether), a farm hand and a maid servant. The farm had six horses, five cows, seven sheep and 14 pigs, and whilst the number of animals remained constant throughout the 19th century, the number of people fluctuated between seven and ten, four of whom were probably maids and farm hands.

The front part of the house stands on a high quarry-stone base. Although the timbering in each of the two storeys in the gable wall is independently framed, the load-bearing posts in the eaves walls and on the inside span the full height of both floors.

The following inscription appears on the bressumer in the upper gable:

Johann Wilhelm Zeddies   Friederica Eleonora
Rensehehausen ANNO 1731

The farm house from the Zeddies farm in Grohnde. The building in the background is the granary belonging to the Valepage farm

The inscription above the door invokes Psalm 37, v. 34 and Psalm 38, v. 8 (Psalm 39 in the Lutheran version)

PS XXXVII VERS 34 HARRE AUF DEN HERREN UND HALTE SEINEN WEG, SO WIRD ER DICH ERHOHEN, DASS DU DAS LAND ERBEST; DU WIR(ST) SEHEN, DASS DIE GOTTLOSEN AUSGEROTTET WERDEN NUN HERR WES SOLL ICH MICH TRÖSTEN, ICH HOFFE AUF DICH PS XXXVIII VERS VIII

Both the pantile cladding on the rear gable and the layout of the interior place this house firmly in the 19th century. At the top of the stone steps and beyond the old front door is the corridor, which was originally open to the roof and must therefore have ressembled a tall, narrow threshing floor. However, some time during the 19th century an intermediate floor was inserted. As regards the use to which the various rooms were put in this period, we have had to rely entirely on information passed on by word of mouth: The four rooms on the left-hand side of the ground floor were living rooms which included a kitchen with an open hearth, a pantry and a servants' chamber, whilst the four rooms on the right comprised a parlour, a living room and two bedrooms (the one at the far end was originally a cow stall). The upper storey contained storage rooms, bedrooms and another living room. At the rear end of the corridor there are a number of doors leading on to the transverse threshing floor, and to the right of it lie the cattle stalls and the stable. The vaulted quarry-stone cellar beneath the parlour was included when the house was first built in 1731.

The large room on the ground floor to the right of the corridor currently accommodates the restaurant "Zum Wilden Mann", and consequently the dividing walls have not been reinstated. The two rooms to the left of the main entrance house the Museum shop where a variety of publications and products of the open air museum can be purchased.

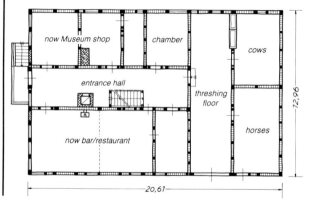

A 15 Barn

from the Zeddies/Kroll farm
in Emmerthal-Kirchohsen
in the district of Hameln-Pyrmont,
built around 1624/30,
dismantled in 1972 and re-erected in 1979 – 80

This barn, which has two aisles and is entered through a door on the left-hand side of the gable wall, was built around 1624 and at that stage consisted of five extremely wide bays. The combination of arch- and tension-braces in the front gable was a common feature of principal buildings in the Weser region during this period. In the 18th century the barn was extended to incorporate a further three smaller bays. It is likely that the slender vertical studs were inserted between the wide wall panels as early as the 18th century to allow the wattle-and-daub infilling to be replaced with stone. During the 19th century the timber-framed pediment of the front gable was weatherboarded, covering the sill on which the remains of an inscription were discovered when the building was being restored. ...Anno 16... Apart from the through passage, the stables were added to the 17th century barn, but these were given up again in favour of cereal stockpiles on ground level, contrary to the usual way of storing in the loft.

Barn of Kirchohsen

A 17 Well

from Schieder in the district of Lippe,
built in the 13th century,
dismantled in 1981 and re-erected in 1982;
and from Höxter-Godelheim
in the district of Höxter,
built in the 19th century,
dismantled and re-erected 1982

The shaft of this well, which is approximately 1.7 metres deep, was sunk in the 12th century, making it the oldest structure in the Museum. It was unearthed in the course of excavation work near Schieder in 1981. To enable it to be transferred to the Museum in one piece, it was encased in a protective sheath.

The curb, on the other hand, was built in the 19th century from ashlar bricks wit rounded corners and originally belonged to a well which served several farmsteads in Godelheim. A wide-angled roof protects the winch with which the water was drawn.

The curb of the well from Godelheim at its original site

A 18 Smithy

Blacksmith Pollmann's farm,
Höxter-Godelheim, district of Höxter,
built in 1777,
dismantled in 1968, re-erected in 1983 – 84

The building accommodating the smithy and its equipment are typical examples of a village smithy in the Paderborn area. Until two generations ago, a village without a smithy would have been unthinkable. The smith was an all-round craftsman taking care of horse shoes, wagons, and carts, and making agricultural implements and forged tools. He was involved in building and construction, supplying fittings, nails, and iron grids. He could repair anything made of iron and was able to run an additional trade selling household goods, metals and tools. His workshop was normally located in the main street, either in the centre of a village or towards the outskirts.

The Pollmann smithy was built in 1777 on the premises of Godelheim no. 14 which are still owned by the Pollmann family.

Towards the end of the 18th century, two Pollmann brothers, Christoph and Heinrich, were employed in neighbouring smithies, working there as smiths. The two workshops were carried on until the sixties of our century, that of the open air museum was run by the succesors of Johann Heinrich Pollmann (1728 – 1805). The two most recent master smiths were Franz Josef Pollmann (1899 – 1972) and his son of same name (1931 – 1976). In the 19th century, the no. 14 premises and smithy included a relatively large estate of 17 acres of farm land and fields. The clientele, the variety of work performed and the production capacity of the workshop are evidenced by pass-books which

Demonstration of smithery in the Pollmann smithy   *1984*

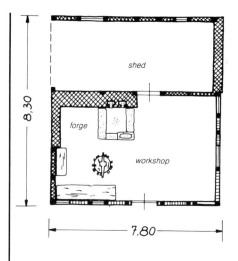

have been handed to the open air museum together with the smithy, covering an almost uninterrupted period from 1832 through 1924. According to the books, the major part of the daily work consisted in repeated horse shoe and repair services. He occasionally applied rims to cart wheels and made plough-shares and axles for carts. From the 1870s onwards, the growing mechaniza-tion of agriculture added new jobs such as for instance whetting machine knives or repairing iron harrows.

The building accommodating the smithy is a half timbered eaves house, approximately 5 meters deep and 7.60 meters long, the walls are 3.10 meters high in addition to the plinth. The rear left corner of the house surrounds the forge and is built of strong Solling quarry stone walls of 40 cm thickness (fire protection). The building is 5 bays wide and rests on wooden sill beams on a variegated sand stone plinth. The low roofed shedlike annex has been reconstructed in the form of a "cart shed" which existed at the smithy as early as 1900.

The smithy was re-erected in the open air museum as it would have been at the turn of the century when the previous forge — which had no chimney — had already been moved out of the dark corner and connected to a more central chimney. Whilst the original smithy was divided up into two rooms, the partition wall was removed later on to gain more room to repair agri-cultural equipment. This modification meant a first step from the mere blacksmithy towards a country blacksmith's work-shop. The blacksmith's tongs, thread cutters, punches, ham-mers, anvil and anvil accessories as well as many other tools, blanks and semi finished products have been passed to the museum together with the Pollmann smithy, or come from comparable country smithies.

A 19 Wayside chapel

Westersporkhof farm,
Rietberg-Westerwiehe, district of Gütersloh,
built in 1697;
dismantled in 1971, re-erected in 1984

Small sacral buildings such as wayside chapels, shrines, or crosses were not mentioned in historical records, except when the authority governing the area or the church exerted an influence on the religious practices of the population. It is, therefore, not surprising not to find the wayside chapel of the Westersporkhof farm in any records, contrary to all other buildings belonging to the farm. We may, however, presume that this wayside chapel was not a place to take processions to.

Small chapels or wayside shrines could be found on many farms. The one of Westerwiehe is a half timbered mini building resting on 3 sqm of ground surface, and is covered by a ridge roof. It was found by a country roadside near the Westersporkhof farm. The slot in the iron box affixed to the backside of the door was a collection box "for the poor and sick". At Christmas and All Saints Day candles were lit inside. The inscription on the front reads:

**O. IESVS. MARIA. IOSEP. BIT. VOR. VNS SVNDER.
AMEN**

Lavishly carved beams, the colours of which were restored according to relevant investigations, decorate the facade of the small house. The gable pediment shows Christ's initials and the cross in a radiating sun.

*Wayside chapel,
altar and pieta*

A 20 The Moven house

from Höxter-Bruchhausen
in the district of Höxter,
built in 1651, dismantled in 1980
and re-erected in 1982 – 86

This house was originally built for Peter Moven and Catherina Trutten, but in 1761 it passed through marriage to the Hesse family, whose property it remained until 1928. The Hesse family lived there until 1877 when they moved into the new house. The old house has since served as an outbuilding. In 1920 it was restored again and let to a train driver.

In 1834 the house presided over 23 hectares of land which was divided up into 50 plots, most of them arable. Some were pastures and meadows. At this point the Hesse family was paying more tax than 95% of the inhabitants of Bruchhausen. Although the amount of land had diminished to a mere 13 hectares by 1838, in 1867 this family was still the fourth most heavily taxed in the district.

The Moven House, with its gable-entry threshing floor serving as a through-passage, is a typical example of the kind commonly found in the Weser region. There is an inscription above the main door which reads:

PETTER MOVEN   **CATHARINA TRVTTEN**
ANNO   1651

At the front of the building on the left-hand side is an outshoot which was designed to provide more space for the parlour. Whilst this is one of the original features of the house, numerous alterations have been made to other parts of the building at various times: The gable pediment, for instance, was originally infilled with wattle-and-daub and did not receive its coat of weatherboarding (presumably because of the cost involved) until the 19th century. In the course of the 18th century the original thatched roof was replaced with a covering of sandstone slates. It is likely that the small room next to the kitchen at the left hand side of the house and the stalls beneath the lean-to roof at the rear of the building were added around the same time. However, the extent of the alterations can perhaps be appreciated more fully from the inside: To begin with, the house consisted only of the threshing floor and the rooms on either side of it. Down the right-hand side were cattle stalls, a stable and, at the far end, what appears to have been a shelter for foals. The space above was used for storing cereals and animal feed. The parlour over on the left was heated by a stove in the kitchen which was not originally closed off from the threshing floor; the smoke from the stone hearth would drift across the threshing floor and up into the loft. Evidence that this was so is provided by the row of curing rods and deposits

The Moven house in Bruchhausen   1980

of soot on the ceiling above the threshing floor.

Around 1800 the kitchen was probably screened off from the threshing floor by a partition underneath the heavy stringer. A flight of steps leads from the kitchen down to a vaulted cellar, above which is a chamber with a low ceiling. On the left hand side of the upper storey are the bedrooms and a smoke-bay. With the exception of the kitchen which has retained its original floor level, all the downstairs rooms were raised by about 40 cm following a flood in the 19th century. Originally there was a lavish covering of peg-top paving at the far end of the threshing floor which was discovered — together with the remains of earlier buildings, probably from the 13th century — in the course of excavation work which took place after the house had been dismantled in 1980. In the Museum the house looks very much as it might have done around 1860.

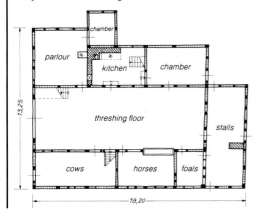

33

A 21–23 Farm and commercial bakery

The small, narrow piece of land was built upon following the pattern of the Hilmer-Borgolte farm in the village of Stahle on the river Weser. Apart from an older farmhouse which was re-erected first, the site included outbuildings which were constructed later in the 19th century, i.e. an attached cow shed, a lavatory at the back side, and a commercial bakehouse. The outbuildings were taken to the open air museum as complete units, partly as entire segments without any dismantling.

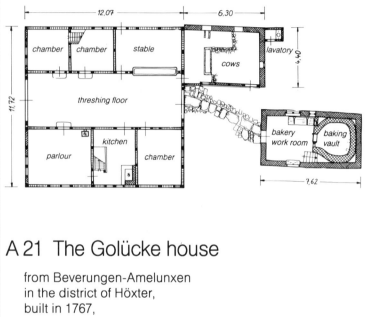

A 21 The Golücke house

from Beverungen-Amelunxen
in the district of Höxter,
built in 1767,
dismantled in 1964 and re-erected in 1976–77

This house was commissioned in 1767 by Johann Dietrich Golücke, whose family had lived in the village of Amelunxen since 1677. In 1834 the farm from which it came possessed a total of 40 acres (10 ha) of mostly arable land. It was certainly large when compared with other village farms in the Weser region, but small when measured against the scattered and isolated farmsteads of Westphalia. During this period the Golücke family was paying more tax than 80% of the population of Amelunxen. At the end of the 18th century the owner's son was described as being "a cottier and a butcher", indicating that he plied a secondary trade as a slaughterman.

The Golücke House is a short, aisled building whose threshing floor stretches from one gable wall to the other. Its high walls are a characteristic feature of buildings from small, tightly-packed villages. The extravagantly constructed front gable with its overhanging upper storey is equally typical of 18th century village architecture in the Weser basin. Some of the panels on this wall are braced with St. Andrew's crosses and infilled with courses of herringbone brick-nogging.

The following four inscriptions also appear on the gable wall:

SO SEGNET GOT DEN   SELBEN MAN DER IHM UM
SEGEN RUFFET AN

ALLES IST AN GOTTES SEEGEN UND AN SEINER
HULD GELEGEN ÜBER ALLES GELD UND GUT
WER AUF GOT SEIN HOFNUNG SETZET DER
BEHALT GANZ UNVERLEZET EINNEN FREIN
HELDEN MUHT

DER MICH BIES HIEHER ERNEHRET UND MIR
MANCHES GLÜK BESCHERET ( ) IST UND BLEIBET
EWICH MEIN WIRD AUCH FORT DER HELFER SEN

AN GOTTES SEGEN IST ALLES GELEGEN WER GOT
VER / TRAUT HAT WOL GEBAUT IM HIMMEL UND
AUF ERDEN / WER SICH VERLÄST AUF IESUM
CHRISTDEN MUSS DER HIMME W (= werden) /
JOHAN DEDRCH GOLLKEN   ANNA CATRINA
SCHLECHT /
ANNO 1767   DEN 15 APR

The Golücke house in Amelunxen   *before 1935*

We can tell that this building is much younger than the Moven House (A 20) by the fact that the living quarters are no longer confined to one side of the ground floor. Moreover, the kitchen, which is situated in the middle of the right-hand aisle, was partitioned off from the threshing floor from the very beginning. The smoke from the open fire was drawn through the smoke-bay overhead and out on to the threshing floor. The only evidence of animal life is provided by the shuttered cow stalls on the left at the far end of the building.

A 22 Cow stalls and lavatory

Hilmer-Borgolte farm,
Höxter-Stahle, district of Höxter,
built prior to 1830;
dismantled in 1983, re-erected in 1984 − 86

The cow shed attached to the farm house of the Hilmer-Borgolte farm in Stahle was slightly advanced at the left eaves wall, and was built up in the same way in the museum behind the Golücke house. The two storey annex partly consists of red Solling stones, partly half timbered walls, and is covered by a steep lean-on roof. At its rear gable, the cesspool is located next to the lavatory. The building was definitely recorded in 1830 for the first time. It normally accommodated two milk cows which were occasionally put to carts. Chaff was kept at the upper floor and hay was stored in the left. The half timbered walls of the stable annex were taken to the open air museum as they were without being dismantled.

A 23 Commercial bakery

Hilmer-Borgolte farm,
Höxter-Stahle, district of Höxter,
built in 1808,
dismantled in 1984 − 85, re-erected in 1985 − 86

At the time of the Napoleonic occupation, the small bakery was opened on a commercial basis. The private baking ovens and bake houses, for which no taxes were paid, had to be taken down according to a governmental decree which had just been passed. In 1812, Stahle counted seven other so called municipal bake houses run under government licence. The bakehouse was run as a secondary trade and chiefly served part of Stahle. It was finally closed in 1941 after having been shut down for several decades in the course of the 19th century. During that time, the building was tenanted as a living quarter recorded as house no. 62 B.

The entrance to the bakery — as it is now in the museum — could only be reached through the short threshing floor of the farmhouse. The bread and cake were sold in one of the front rooms on the ground floor of the farm house, at least in the 20th century, not every day, merely on some special days of the week. The farmyard between the farmhouse and the bakehouse is largely paved. A chicken fence was installed — as long as required — between the cow shed and the bakehouse to keep the poultry away. At the two corners of the cow shed and the bakery, traces of the agricultural vehicles can still be seen, as they were squeezed onto the farmyard from behind.

Commercial bakehouse (on the left) and cow shed (on the right) behind the farmhouse at the original site, 1983.

On the ground floor, the bakehouse is built of red Solling sandstone with a half timbered storey on top, infilled with brick. This upper floor was taken to the open air museum in one large piece, including the clay ceiling. The ground floor is divided into the workroom and the large vault which was re-erected in its present form late in the 19th century in lieu of a previous model. When this last oven was built in, the front upper chamber was removed and the chimney was put on an iron girder. The niches right and left of the oven mouth were used to keep things warm. The sparse furniture such as a table and shelves as well as the very few gadgets show that the oven was mainly used to bake the bread and cake the village people had prepared themselves and had it baked against a charge. Very often, not even the dough was made in the workroom of the bakehouse. Most of the bread was made of rye. The oven vault took approximately 40 loaves at a time.

From the workroom, stone steps lead across the oven wall up to the adjacent upper floor which may date back to the year of construction. The chamber on this floor was located on top of the baking vault and was lit by two small windows. For the last few years it was used to let the dough rise.

A 24 – 26 Manor house

This group of buildings comprises a manor house (Schönhof), a shed and a small summerhouse which is situated on an escarpment wall between the baroque garden and the lower lying orchard.

A 24 The Schönhof

from Wiedenbrück in the district of Gütersloh, built around 1720, dismantled in 1968 and re-erected between 1973 – 75

On 11 February 1712 Franz Wilhelm Harsewinkel, the chief administrator of Reckenberg, based in Osnabrück, was invested with the Schönhof estate in Wiedenbrück. The chief entitled him to a share of the taxes from the town of Wiedenbrück and a number of the surrounding farms. This investment enraged the local judge, Heinrich Kothe, who claimed that a large part of the land included in the fief belonged to him. When Harsewinkel attempted to use his public office to draw the King of Prussia into the dispute he was dismissed. Nonetheless, he eventually succeeded in purchasing the Schönhof in 1721. Several generations later the estate was inherited by the district treasurer, Franz Wilhelm Harsewinkel (the younger). In 1774 he leased it to his brother, Karl Florenz Harsewinkel, dean of the collegiate chapter of Wiedenbrück who completely renovated the house, lavishing particular attention: on the large banqueting hall (Schönhof-Saal).

The Schönhof from Wiedenbrück

The builder of the Schönhof
Description on the reverse of the painting:
„Franziskus Wilhelmus Harsewinkel Quaestor in Reckenberg
Aetatis 50 1708"

The extremely valuable collection of paintings amassed by the dean is known to have included works by Albrecht Dürer, Hans Holbein, Lucas Cranach, Jacob Ruisdael, Peter Paul Rubens, Titian and Paolo Veronese. In 1795 the entire collection was sold to someone in Petersburg, save for a handful of comparatively plain paintings and a selection of portraits of members of the Harsewinkel family, some of which can still be seen in the Schönhof. In 1854, as a consequence of marriage, the house became the property of the Uhle family.

The house was situated on the outskirts of Wiedenbrück near the castle, which later became the administrative centre of Reckenberg. In 1968 it had to make way for a new road scheme.

The Schönhof is an exceptionally long building with a half-hipped gable roof and its eaves walls parallel to the street. It dates from the 17th century and around 1700 it became the lord of the manor's residence. Its facade is a picture of symmetry. Either side of the central door each alternate vertical

panel houses two windows, one serving the upper storey and

one the ground floor. The door itself is adorned with a beautiful late-baroque fanlight. The large portal in the front gable gives on to the threshing floor, and this section of the building differs little from most other farmhouses in Westphalia.

The door in the eaves wall leads into a small lobby the plinth of which is painted in a marble pattern. The door on the right provides access to a suite of three heated rooms. Straight ahead is a baroque staircase leading to the upper floor, whilst the door on the left leads into the kitchen. This rather peculiar layout was the price that had to be paid for having the front door sited in the centre of the facade.

A

The kitchen of the Schönhof in Wiedenbrück   *1963*

The kitchen, which is open to the rafters, is separated from the threshing floor by a timber-framed wall. As in all old farmhouses it was a multipurpose domestic work room. The original fireplace was removed when the house was renovated and it has been replaced in the Museum with one made in 1705 from the Meier Osthoff farm in Harsewinkel. As a key room to the building, the kitchen also has certain representative functions. It contains a number of ancestral portraits and several paintings which belonged to the Schönhof, and on the chimney breast there is a pictorial representation of Jacob's Dream (The Ladder to Heaven).

The door to the left of the fireplace leads into the drawing room. In the extreme right hand corner there is a narrow passage containing a washing bay which extends as far as the rear eaves wall.

Schönhof hall   *around 1965*

Schönhof
Details of the wall
paintings during the
restoration: Herakles,
puttoes and bacchanals

Here, too, are the steps leading down, to the cellar. Over on the right hand side of the kitchen are the dining room and crockery store. The short staircase to the right of the fireplace leads up to the "Schönhof Room", the banqueting hall with its magnificent wall and ceiling paintings. The ceiling is decorated in typical rococo style and the picture at its centre is a perspective view through a window into a clouded sky in which

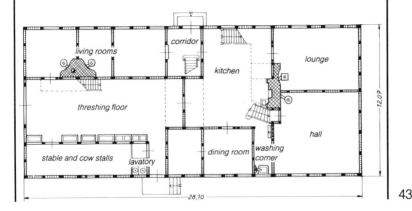

43

the goddess Athena is floating. The painted moulding between the walls and the ceiling and the wall paintings themselves are slightly more recent in style. Going by the signature of the artist and the date **(Rosenckrant Fec 1796),** they did not appear until after the sale of the important collection of paintings. The walls are divided into sections by pilasters painted in a marble pattern, crowned with ionic capitals and garlands of fruit and circumscribed by an illusionistic "entablature" adorned with allegories ot the Four Arts. The decorations in the wall panels draw on the Pompeiian tradition.

Almost all the fixtures and fittings in this room are the original ones, including the late 18th century furniture from the workshop of Philipp Ferdinand Bartscher from Rietberg. The two small chambers above the dining room are the servants' quarters, whilst those above the living rooms comprise the dean's bedroom suite. The blue wall-hangings in the two front bedrooms were recreated from remnants which were discovered when the building was being dismantled.

A 25 Shed

from Schlangen-Kohlstädt
in the district of Lippe,
built in 1835, dismantled in 1978
and re-erected in 1979

This shed was erected in 1835 as a fire station to serve the community of Kohlstädt, and its design formed the basis for a number of other new fire stations which were built at the time. It is a single-storey timber-framed building with a gable door, which today houses the heating plant on which the Schönhof relies for its continued preservation.

*Fire station
(now shed)
in Kohlstädt
1978*

*Picture to
the right
summerhouse
prior to being
dismantled
in 1981*

A 26 Summerhouse

from the Maygadessen Estate
in Höxter-Godelheim in the district of Höxter,
built in the 18th century,
dismantled and re-erected in 1981

In the 18th and 19th centuries most of the estates belonging to
the nobility, the clergy and the bourgeoisie had summer-
houses, but few of them have survived. This octagonal summerhouse, which contains a cellar, was built as an open-sided
pavilion, although one row of infilled panels was decorated
with St. Andrews crosses. At the time it was largely constructed of timber taken from an older house. However, when the
building was altered in 1842/46 its sides were sealed with
quarry-stone and large leaded windows were installed. These
were replaced with smaller ones during the course of further
alterations which were carried out at the end of the 19th century.

A 28 The Stahl house

The Hoffbauer/Stahl house, from
Gütersloh/district of Gütersloh,
built in 1730;
dismantled in 1971, re-erected in 1982 – 86

Gütersloh, Stahl house at the Domhof, coloured postcard about 1910

The distiller's house was commissioned by the merchant Peter Friedrich Hoff-bauer and his wife Christina Dorothea, née Pollwort, as witnessed by the inscription above the door.

Jesu las uns auf der Erden. Nichtes suchen als allein.
Das Du mögest bey uns Sein und wir Dir mögn ähnlich werden
in dem Leben dieser Zeit und in Jener Ewigkeit.
Peter Frich Hoffbaur   Christina Dorotea Pollwort
anno 1730   den 10. May
M. J. KM

Peter Friedrich Hoffbauer traded in iron goods and tapped spirits. As recorded in the official books of 1729 and 1730, tapping liquor was fairly common among the Gütersloh citizens. On March 31, 1730, 46 inhabitants of Gütersloh were fined because they sold liquor after hours, i.e. later than allowed. One of them was Peter Friedrich Hoffbauer.
After his death (presumably about 1740), his widow married her cousin Hermann Christian Betke of Rinteln. The couple commissioned the two aisled annex. The door of the annex shows the following inscription:

ALLES IST AN GOTTES SEGEN UND AN SEINER GNADE GELEGEN / HERMANN CHRISTIAN BETKE CHRISTINA DOROTHEA BETKE G. POLLWORTH / ANNO 1748 DEN 1 AUGUST / M CHRISTIAN ZUR MÜHLEN

Next to the door a lavatory is added to the annex. It was taken from the rear side of a house in the village Amelgatzen. In 1790 the granddaughter of the builder, Dorothea Margarethe Hoffbauer (1770 – 1818) was married to Johann Heinrich Stahl (1761 – 1832), son of a pastor from the Sauerland. The house and shop were then carried on under the name of Stahl.

The building is a relatively short, high walled four post and beam structure with a gable pediment jettied twice on adorned tie beams. On the sill of the gable pediment we read:

Anfang und Ende in allen meinen Sachen laß mich jederzeit mit dir meinen Gott und Schöpfer machen – wer Gott vertraut hat wohlgebaut im Himmel und auf Erden wer sich verläßt auf Jesum Christ dem mus der Himmel werden.

The Gütersloh town farmer's house became famous for its valuable richly decorated two wings roccoco door with its lavishly ornate upper window giving light to the threshing floor. The main door was built in around 1790 by Johann Heinrich Stahl together with the inside partition which was given windows to let the light in, and several inside doors and wall cabinets.
After the death of Johann Heinrich Stahl, his youngest daughter Charlotte Amalie inherited the house, whilst the youngest son Carl Christoph (1808 – 1865) was given his father's shop.

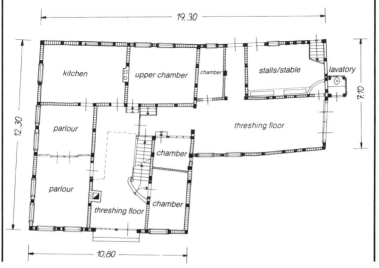

Rococo portal (about 1790) within the arch of 1730

In 1837 Carl Christoph Stahl rented his sister's house and together with the dispenser Carl Pfennig he founded the "Domhof wine distillers Carl Stahl". When Pfennig had left the business again, Stahl carried on alone. He made corn brandy, gin and liqueurs, and traded in spices.

In 1848 Stahl bought the house from his sister for 2000 Taler and lived in it together with his second wife Pauline Wilhelmine Menge.

The house in the museum is furnished as it would have been around 1860. At the back and sides, the threshing floor is surrounded by living rooms. A gallery provides access to the rooms on the upper floor. On the ground floor, two rooms are at the left of the entrance, separated by the rococo wing door added in 1790. The room further back is next to the kitchen. At the right of the adjacent upper chamber a passage leads to the threshing floor of the 1748 annex. There are some bedrooms on the upper floor (the smoking chamber, too, is supposed to have been on this floor).

The liquor was not made in the house, but in a barn on the farmyard, whereas the shop was most probably kept in the farmhouse. The cellar underneath the upper chamber and the room to the right of the staircase were used for storage, i.e. the liquor and other goods were kept in barrels well protected from vermin and humidity.

A

A 29 The Brigitte house

from Rietberg in the district of Gütersloh,
built in 1602;
dismantled in 1974, re-erected in 1985 – 86

According to the inscription, Jost Kleine built the granary in 1602 on a farm-stead adjacent to the churchyard. Some time in the 18th century, the civil servant Reinking's family acquired the entire premises. In 1776, Reinking was appointed Councillor or the Exchequer in the county of Rietberg, i.e. an office previously held by his father. That very year, he had the farmhouse and the granary modified, turning the granary into a residential outbuilding. In her last will written in 1837, his widow mentions the name "Brigitte house" for the first time, but nobody has ever been able to find any explanation for the name. Daughter Lisette Klee inherited the farm house and let it to several civil servants and their families, and even the small Brigitte house was occupied, presumably by a day labourer's family of eight around 1840. From 1891 on-wards, the tenants were the 62 years old single seamstress Katharina Kleinegesse and the widow of the court messenger Wiedemeier, the two living there in a two persons household. In 1894/95 the former acquired the house together with her two sisters. When she had died, the heirs sold the small house to the church warden of the Roman Catholic church who in turn let it to the labourer Heinrich Pickstroer.

The two storey half timbered eaves house, resting on a ground surface of not quite 36 sqm. is jettied on three sides of the upper floor and roof. The web members between the storeys show a very modern carved chevron design. The lower headrail of the right hand gable shows the following inscription:

49

Der cxxvii psam Martinis Docto(r)is Lutheri vorgeben ist alle muh und kost wo gott nitt selber das Haus bauwet also ist der mensch trost loeß wo ehr seine eigen kraften trawt / den wo (die stat) got nit mit seinem rath nit selbst erhelt noch schütcet man wacht ohne gots gut vor war sulchs ni nutz Jost kleine me fieri (?) fecit AN: 602 Die 28 MARTII

The translation reads: The 127th psalm according to Doctor Martin Luther: In vain are all efforts and cost where God Himself does not build the house, for man is dismal where he (only) trusts in his own strength / because where God does not Himself maintain and protect (the place) under his council, one wakes without God's kindness (and) such would be of no avail. Jost Kleine made me . . . in the year 1602 on March 23.

Brigitte house with its small front garden

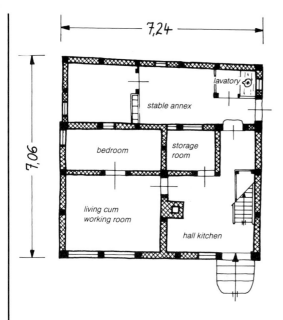

As Rietberg returned to the catholic faith, this reformed inscription which could be read from the churchyard was covered up with a thick coat of paint and rediscovered in the open air museum.

The visitor to the Brigitte house passes through a narrow front garden which — according to its condition in 1891 — is laid out for two different tenants. The present entrance was made as late as in the 19th century. The stairs to the upper floor were turned around by 180°. The major part of the windows as well dates back to this period of reconstruction. The original entrance is in the rear eaves wall and now leads into the stable annex. In Rietberg, the annex no longer existed, but could be reconstructed according to a taxation description on 1875, including a goats shed and a lavatory.

The kitchen in the hall and the small storage room were shared by the tenants. The room at the ground floor — lit by large windows — is a living cum working room and was used by the seamstress who presumably worked at home. Next to it is the bedroom which is only 1.50 m wide. The upper floor was occupied by a widow and her son. On this floor, the living rooms and bedrooms were subdivided by a mere wood partition. The same applies to the division of the bedroom to the left of the staircase. The rooms are wallpapered as indicated in the building reports, the furniture of the bedroom and living room are from the period.

A 31 Farm house

Finkeldei-Arnecke,
Emmerthal-Grohnde, district of Hameln-Pyrmont,
built in 1622, reconstructed in 1909;
dismantled in 1972, re-erected in 1989 – 90

In Grohnde, the house was built in 1622 and stood next to the village pond, and so it stands in the museum. First built as a classical through passage house for one family, it was occupied by three families for some time at the end of the 19th century. At the time, a baking oven existed in the annex, but was no longer there when the first reports of the building supervision were written in 1905. In that year, mention is made of a stable annex which was constructed of solid stones and was to have a pantile roof, contrary to the main house with its timber framed walls and Solling stone roof covering. In 1907, the house passed into the ownership of the Arnecke family. The road warden and tenant innkeeper Conrad Arnecke had the house reconstructed in 1909 and divided even the threshing floor into two floors.

In its present form, the four post and beam house with its original through passage threshing floor bears the imprint of reconstruction in 1909. The slightly lowered transom above the two wing entrance door (instead of the former large door to the threshing floor) carries this inscription:

CORDT FINCKELDIE ET YLSABE WEIBKEN
ANNO   1622

The Finckeldei-Arnecke house at its original site   *1971*

52

The representative extension to the parlour shows two friezes carved in a chevron design, ornamental chamfers and inscriptions:

WAS MICH DIE LEVTE GÖNNE DAS GÖNE IHN GOT WIDER wir bauwen alle veste und seindt doch keine bleibende geste

Two of the former three richly decorated parapet plates of the late renaissance period showing symbols of crafts and trades were removed in favour of larger windows. And yet, the extension was the reason why the house has been re-erected in the open air museum. Extensions of his type are very typical of the renaissance buildings along the river Weser, and are frequently found with castles as well as with farm houses.

The two lateral aisles are different in width. In its original state, the narrow left hand aisle on the ground floor served as a stable and feeding passage, whereas the right hand aisle was used to live in. At the turn of the last century, the stable had to make way for more living space. The left hand aisle was changed into a narrow parlour at the front gable, a kitchen behind it, and a chamber: In the right hand aisle — as before — we find the parlour which is particularly comfortable through the extension, a kitchen behind it — the original kitchen of the house — and a second parlour instead of a chamber at the rear end. The two living quarters included bedrooms on the upper floor ever since the threshing floor had been divided into two stories; a third family lived in the former bakehouse which was turned into a stable at a later date.

A 34 The Ludovici house

Bad Driburg-Neuenheerse, district of Höxter,
built in 1608 — 14, reconstructed in 1777;
dismantled in 1969, re-erected in 1986 — 89

Theodor Ludovici, distributor (secretary of the chapter) of the Ladies' Foundation of Neuenheerse was the builder of the farm house in 1608 to 1614. The house changed ownership early in the 18th century and was empty around 1770. In 1777 it underwent comprehensive repair work. It was then owned by the Fasner family which was also linked with the Ladies' Foundation. By the middle of the 19th century, it had been left to decay again. The day labourer Kasper Gehlhaus who had become the owner by marriage tried to set it on fire to cash the sum insured. His leasehold was terminated and he was sentenced to jail in Münster. In 1852, Johann Konrad Stork took over the farm; he thoroughly refurbished the buildings. In the 18th century, the farm had included 70 acres of land, by the end of the 19th century it had grown to 100 acres. The last owners were the Weskamp family.

The arch of the doorway of Ludovici house when re-erected   1986

The Ludovici house comprises a large four post and beam farm building. Instead of a living area inside the building, a narrow annex is added at the backside on a vaulted cellar which is only slightly sunk into the ground. The figures on the tie beam tells the beginning and end of the building activities which covered six years in total, a fact which has been proved in an additional dendochronological analysis. At the front gable, the gable pediment is jettied twice on dragon beams. The web members and sills together with the delicate pearl-string and T-shaped ornamentation and the inscriptions add up to distinct ornamental friezes. On the very strong doorframe, the inscriptions above the ornaments flat cut in the renaissance style are another decorative element. A year appears at the arch:

IHS   AN : DO: MRIA.
                      1614
PAX: INTRANTIBVS: SALVS: EXEVNTIBVS ·
THEOD: LVDOVICI: GERTRVD: WESTRM:
CONIVGES.

The inscription on the crossbeam of the gable pediment:

NISI DOMINVS · A DIFICAVERIT · DOMVM ·
FRVSTRA · LABORAVERVNT · QVI AEDIFI CANT ·
EAM · NISI · DOMIN · CVSTODIERIT · CIVITATEM ·
FRVSTRA · VIGILAT · QVI · CVSTODIT · EAM
PSALM 126

Today the threshing floor looks as it did after the changes made in the 18th century: The left hand wall of the threshing floor was advanced to make the stable aisle wider. Originally,

54

this aisle accommodated the cow stalls and had an extension bay at its end. At this occasion, the wall towards the right hand aisle was partly renewed. A peculiarity of this wall is the upper floor which is jettied into the threshing floor, the jettied part is decorated with a simple renaissance pattern. This rear part of the right aisle obviously served for living purposes, whereas the front part originally housed stables. At the end of the threshing floor, the two upper floors of the aisles are connected by a simple baroque gallery which can be reached by stairs on top of the cellar staircase. The stairs leading down into the cellar are advanced into the threshing floor in rather a strange way, and are crowned by a portal of ashlar stone dated 1608. Its mullions are rooted in the gothic tradition. The inscription reads:

$$M \cdot H \cdot Z \cdot G \cdot D \cdot L \cdot A \cdot D \cdot 1608$$

This may stand for the name and style of the master builder (M.H.Z.G.), the abbreviation of the man's name for whom the house was built (Dietrich Ludowigs), and for Anno Domini. The rear hall structure resting on the strong walls of a barrel vaulted cellar was renewed in 1787. At this occasion the timber framed storey was built with a hall in the middle and smaller lateral rooms.

A 59 Craftsman's house

Neue Torstraße 10,
Blomberg, district of Lippe,
built in 1450 and 1610;
dismantled in 1968, re-erected in 1986 – 89

The various owners of the town farmer's house of Blomberg can be traced back to 1671 when Lucas Schröder acquired the building. The subsequent owners were several craftsmen, among them the joiner Casimir Rose from 1742 onwards, and another joiner, Karl-August-Friedrich-Philipp Schmidt from 1872 onwards.
The relatively small craftsmen's and town farmers' house is very old. Parts of the binders and joists and the roof structure date back to 1450, so that it counts among the oldest timber framed buildings in East Westphalia. In 1550, the building was reconstructed for the first time, in 1610 the entire wall unit underneath the roof structure – which obviously remained – was renewed. At this occasion, the richly carved late renaissance facade was added. This was the reason why the aisle – which was very narrow originally – was made wider on three window axes on top of a wide window bay. However, the door first remained in the middle of the threshing floor – thus further to the right – and was moved further to the left when the house was reconstructed again in 1865 when damage to the foundations had to be repaired.

The facade is now what it was at the turn of the century and has lost much of its original renaissance form: At the door the braces have been cut, the batten bearing the inscriptions was removed, the entire door was lined and faced. The rich carvings outside the parlour have disappeared due to the structural changes, except for some on the wide nogging on top of the ground floor windows. A number of ornamental battens which once protruded from the facade were removed in the 19th century.

Inside as well, much repair work had been performed. The kitchen part was made smaller in 1727, the hall was renovated in 1742, and half of a post in the threshing floor was replaced in 1780. These changes partly coincide with the change of owners: In 1727, Heinrich Pustcocke, in 1742 the aforementioned joiner Casimir Rose, and in 1781 the brick master Georg Wilhelm Plöger acquired the house. It seems as if each new owner first had to repair the building. In this way, each generation has left its traces. The threshing floor is accompanied by one aisle only, containing a parlour and a chamber on the ground floor as well as the kitchen which was once open towards the threshing floor. At the back of it, a hall and a vaulted cellar are attached in the full width of the house, providing a lateral entrance from the farmyard. A ceiling was inserted in the originally high hall which was used as a workshop by joiner Schmidt towards the end of the 19th century. Schmidt used the rooms on the ground floor the way his predecessors did, i.e. parlour, chamber and kitchen where the smoke of the stove freely escaped through the threshing floor until 1913. At the side of the passage towards the farmyard, the joiner kept two cows and two pigs in stalls.

The upper floor, though merely 1.80 m high, was increasingly used for living, and the originally narrow gallery was extended beyond the open space above the living area.

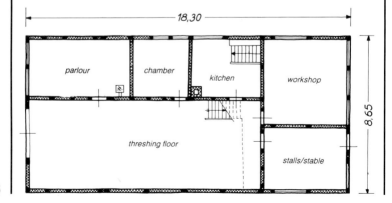

Craftsman's house in Blomberg, Neue Torstraße 10   *around 1964*

A 60 Town farmer's house

Düsterdieck-Kumlehn house,
Mittlere Straße 11,
Holzminden, district of Holzminden,
built in 1677;
dismantled in 1969, re-erected in 1984 – 87

The house which was built in Holzminden by Hans-Conrad Düsterdiek in 1677 was extended by approximately one third at the rear early in the 19th century at the latest. At that time, the house was already owned by the Kumlehn family (1754 – 1966), though more detailed information about the inhabitants is only known from the 20th century when the owner himself, or retired farmers, lived in it. It was tenanted from 1936 onwards.

The subdivision of the large four post and beam structure can be seen from outside: A wide left hand aisle, a high and narrow threshing floor and a narrow aisle to the right. This is a high walled post and beam building with the upper floors of the aisles jettied on dragon beams in the way of multi storied structures. The same applies to the gable pediment, the lower part of which is underlined by a frieze type pattern of inclined braces on all posts. The front gable was constructed in its present form around 1900. The original steep gable was turned into a half hipped roof, the brick infills are underlined by red and white paint. A row of wide windows admits light to the room on the ground floor. The main door is very picturesque with its twisted side posts and a long ornamental inscription.

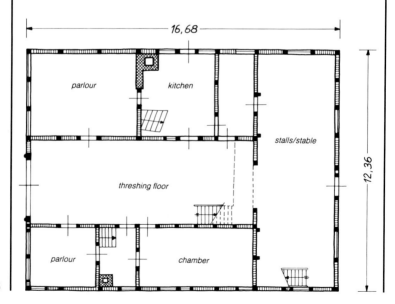

Town farmer's house in Holzminden, Mittlere Straße 11   *1969*

O GOTT, DER DU DAS GRAS SO SCHON IN
FELDERN ZIEREST,
DEN VOGELN WUNDERLICH DIE SPEISE SELBST
ZUFÜHREST,
DU WIRST MIR, DER ICH BIN DEIN KIND, SO VIEL
BESCHEREN,
DAS ICH NACH NOTHDURFT MICH KAN
KLEIDEN UND ERNEHREN.
HANS CONRAD DUSTERDIECK · 1677 · DE 6. 8BRIS
ANNA MARIA DUSTERDIECK · GEBO · HARMANIN

Inscriptions are worked into the bressumer of the gable pediment as well as into the cross beams between the different stories:

WIER BAUWEN HIER ALLE STEIF UND FESTE
UND SEIND ALHIER NUR FROMDE GESTE
UND DA WIER SOLTEN EWIG SEIN
DA BAUWEN WIER GAR WENIG DREIN
HIER BAUW ICH NUR EIN NEST IM HIMMEL ABER
FEST

WIRF DEIN ANLIGEN AUFDEN HERREN DER
WIRD DICH VERSORGEN

Inside the building, the high through passage threshing floor has been kept unobstructed, the half timbered walls have remained unplastered. The living rooms have always been in the large left hand aisle on the ground floor: In front, the parlour above the vaulted cellar, the kitchen behind it, followed by the chamber. In the narrow right hand aisle the front room was also a parlour, but this time on the joist ceiling of a cellar which was built in at a later date. The narrow kitchen adjacent to this parlour was presumably installed in the 19th century, when more room was wanted for a second family. The stalls and stables used to be immediately behind, but these were soon moved to the annex attached to the rear in the full width of the building. We do not know whether the rooms on the upper floor of the aisles were living rooms from the very beginning.

A 61 Fire station

from Lügde-Hummersen
in the district of Lippe,
built in 1839,
dismantled in 1974 and re-erected in 1979

Until well into the 18th century country fires were fateful events for which the primitive fire-fighting equipment (leather buckets and simple hand pumps) was no match at all. Furthermore, there was no centrally organised fire service. However, in 1801 a law was passed in the Lippe region which required every

The fire station at Hummersen   *1974*

village to have its own fire-fighting pump and to set aside a building where it could he housed. A large number of fire stations were built after 1830, such as the one in Hummersen, which was erected following a large fire in 1838. The fire stations at Evenhausen, Kachtenhausen, Lipperode and Kohlstädt were all based on the same design.

The modest exterior of this building reflects its purely utilitarian purpose as a store for fire-fighting equipment. It is a single-storey, one-room building with large double doors in the gable wall. Angle braces at all four corners help stabilise the timber frame. The only feature of any note is the roof. Whereas the majority of fire-stations have tiled roofs, this particular one has a covering of sandstone slates. The fire station contains hoses, buckets, ladders and two fire wagons: the horse-drawn wagon was made in 1804 and came from the village of Eversberg, whilst one of the pumps came from the "Provinzialheilanstalt Warstein" and was manufactured by the firm of "Höing & Plug GmbH, Feuerlöschgeräthe-Fabrik, Cöln/Rhein".

A 80 Chapel

from the Meiwes Farm in Delbrück-Westenholz
in the district of Paderborn,
probably built in 1775,
dismantled in 1979 and re-erected in 1980 – 81

This small half-timbered chapel was built at the edge of a wood bordering the Meiwes farm in Westenholz near Delbrück, probably in 1775. In 1789 the owner of the farm sought permission from the church to hold a thanks-giving procession from Westenholz to the chapel. This procession, which was dedicated to St. Peter and St. Paul, took place every year on 29 June or the following Sunday, until the 1960s.

The porch which leads into the small prayer room is retained by four octagonal wooden pillars. The outdoor pulpit was used by the preacher at the end of the procession.
The side walls of the chapel are furnished with a series of parallel diagonal angle braces whose function is more decorative than structural. This type of bracing was quite common in central Germany in the 18th century, particularly in the area around (East Hessia/Thuringia).

Chapel from Westenholz

C   The Sauerland village

A small hamlet like village of about 30 buildings is being erected in the West-phalian Open Air Museum, dedicated to the Sauerland as a partial region in the Southwest of Westphalia. It nestles in a flat basin remeniscent of the forest covered and slightly hilly highland of the Sauerland. The Sauerland village is under construction, but not yet open to the public.

The arrangement of the village follows the pattern of the small villages of the old districts of Meschede and Olpe. It will include buildings from the former county of Mark (hence "Märkisches Sauerland") as well as from large parts of the former duchy of Westphalia which belonged to the electorate of Cologne (hence "Kurkölnisches Sauerland"), today called Hochsauerland (high Sauer-land). The Eastern part of the area borders the former bishopric of Paderborn. Influences from the Bergische Land (hilly land between the rivers Ruhr and Sieg) and from Hessia are noticeable and visible in varying intensities in · connection with the different ways of settling, building and living.

The economic development of the Sauerland was essentially coined by relatively sterile soil and a permanent abundance of wood and water. Natural resources gave rise to an early small iron industry and widespread charcoal burner's camps. Household goods made of wood were distributed through a migrating trade. Agriculture consisted of a field and grass system, the farmers grew oats and kept relatively large herds of cattle.

Several buildings of varying social origin reveal the social structure of the small Sauerland villages. Next to the large and high ornamental gables of the early four post and beam farmhouses we find smaller houses of more recent times in which the threshing floors are transversal.

C 1 Farm house

Kayser-Henke farm,
Finnentrop-Ostentrop, district of Olpe,
built in 1770;
dismantled in 1972, re-erected in 1986 – 90

The high walled half timbered farmhouse on a quarry stone plinth stood in Ostentrop no. 8 as a central farm building. This is a village in the parish of Schönholthausen counting 280 inhabitants in 1819. Very early the house was described as a remarkable architectural monument of the Sauerland, partly because of its richly decorated gable. In the 18th and 19th centuries, the Kayser farm (Henke since 1790) employed more domestic servants at times than were found on all other farms of the village. In the 19th century the economic conditions were obviously worse.

The arch above the door tells the date of construction:

4. Jully 1770

and the couple who had it built:

Johannes Georgius Kayser und Maria Elisabeth Keyser   63

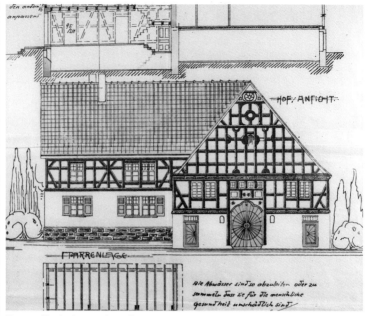

Kayser-Henke house from Ostentrop, reconstruction plan   1925

The inscription on the bressumer of the gable pediment calls to St. John against sin and shame, to St. Agatha against fire and flames and to St. Xaver against hail and thunderbolt. Woodcarved baroque statues of the saints stand in the niches right and left of the entrance door to the threshing floor and in the centre of the gable pediment. The inscription reads:

ALLMÆCHTIGER GOTT UNS UNTTER
STVZE: DURCH SANCT MARJÆ UNS
BESCHVZE: SANCT JOHANNIS FVR
SVNDT UND SCHANDT · S · AGATÆ
FVR FEUER UND BRAND · S · XAVERii ·
FVR HAGEL UND DONNER STREICH:
UND ERWERBEN · MÖGEN · DAS ·
HIMMELREICHSCASPAR · MELCHIOR ·
BALTASAR · VND PATRONN · UNSERER ·
PFAHR · BEHVTET UNS FVR ALLER GEFAHR

E 1 – 7 Mills

E 1 – 3 Tower mill and associated buildings

Most windmills were situated outside or at the edge of towns and villages. They were positioned well away from other buildings and trees to avoid the wind being deflected from their sails, and this explains why the subsidiary buildings in the Museum — the barn and the miller's house (planned) — stand south of the windmill.

The miller was an artisan, and due to the unpredictable nature of his work he was considered in some quarters to be "dishonourable". Depending on the wind conditions, he might not be able to mill any corn at all for days on end, whereas at other times he would be working at full stretch, sometimes well into the night. It was customary for the miller to have a subsidiary trade in addition to his primary craft.

E 1 Tower mill

The Schaaf/Döpke mill
from Rahden-Tonnenheide
in the district of Minden-Lübbecke,
built in 1789/1842, dismantled in 1966
and re-erected between 1974 and 1978

This tower mill was built in Tonnenheide near Rahden on the border with Lower Saxony in 1789. It was privately owned and was erected with the permission of the government of the Kingdom of Prussia which was anxious to ensure that the local farmers did not take their corn to be ground at the "foreign" mill in the neighbouring Hannoverian town of Diepenau. However, in 1842 the Tonnenheide mill is reputed to have fallen victim to an arson attack and it is assumed that the entire wooden structure had to be replaced. Surprisingly, when it was reconstructed none of the recent technical innovations such as the fan-tail, which automatically turned the sails into the wind, was incorporated. In fact the mill was only employed to about a quarter of its potential capacity in the ensuing period — the competition from the neighbouring mills was so great that any investment in more advanced technology would not have been recouped. This particular windmill was still in use in 1952.

In contrast to the post mill, the cap of the tower mill on which the sails are mounted rotates above a fixed tower like structure. The Tonnenheide mill consists of an octagonal wooden frame which is supported on a base of quarrystone pillars and brickwork. One section of wall carries two inscription plates on which the dates 1789 and 1842 are engraved. The passageway in the base allowed the farmers to drive their carts directly underneath the mill. Standing on the wooden stage, the miller would turn the sails into the wind with the aid of the tail pole.
The mill is divided into five floors: the dust floor (first floor), the stone floor, and two machine floors, and finally the cap of the tower. The tower itself has a height of 15 metres; if one includes the sails, which are 20 metres in diameter, the total height of the mill is 25 metres. The wooden frame of the tower is reinforced with a series of cross-shaped braces and horizontal beams. These beams or joists also support the various floors. The external timbers are protected by an outer shell composed of more than 12,000 oak shingles.
The gears: The sails turn an inclined windshaft on which a powerful wooden brake wheel measuring 2½ metres in diameter is mounted. The cogs of the brake wheel engage the horizontal wallower which in turn drives a vertical spindle known as the "main shaft". To this is attached the great spur wheel, which has a diameter of 2.73 metres. To set the milling process in operation, the miller has to bring the spindles on which the two sets of stones are mounted into contact with the great spur wheel by hand.

The tower mill of Tonnenheide

The grinding operation: Using the sack hoist, the miller winches the corn on to the stone floor (i.e. the 2nd floor) and then pours into one of the hoppers which feed the two sets of millstones (one set is equipped with a "bolter" for dressing the flour out of the meal, whilst the other (behind the stairs) is used for producing coarse meal or "grist". When the spindles rotate they not only operate the runner stones but also strike against the feed shoe, which in turn shakes the grain out of the hopper on to the stones. The grain trickles slowly between the two stones where it is then ground. The face of each stone is dressed with grooves which gradually push the meal out towards the "tun" or wooden casing surrounding the stones. From here it falls through the meal spout into either a sack or the "bolter". The sacks can be attached directly to the meal spout to prevent the descending meal missing its target. If the meal is to be "dressed" (i.e. turned into flour) it is passed through 3 sieves of different mesh width, so that the finer meal can be separeted from the grist, which is then milled again until it meets the required standard.

E 2 Barn

from Herten Castle, Herten,
in the district of Recklinghausen,
built in 1695;
dismantled in 1976 and re-erected in 1978

This timber-framed building was originally situated in the court-yard of Herten castle where it served as a barn, stable and cowshed in the late 18th and 19th centuries.

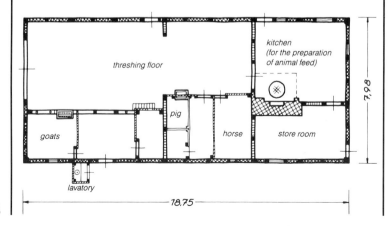

The barn from Herten before being dismantled 1976

In terms of its construction, this barn is typical of many others to be found along the Western Hellweg. The scissor bracing in the eaves walls is a particularly characteristic feature. Its hipped roof is covered with tiles. The inscription over the door reads:

EXSTRUCTUM EST
ANNO 1695   den 6 IULY

The structural alterations which were carried out in the 19th century can be seen more clearly on the inside. In fact all that remains of the original building is the transverse wall in which an archway has been cut. Initially, then, the barn comprised only two large rooms, one at the front and one at the rear. Subsequently, the right hand side of the threshing floor was sectioned off and turned into stalls for cows and goats. Hens were kept in the loft, which was also used for storing hay and straw. The space beyond the archway was divided into four rooms which, among other things, contained a stable, a pigsty and a food preparation area complete with a fireplace. A lavatory has been built on to the right hand eaves wall.

E 3 Miller's house

(planned)

E 4 Post mill

The Pape mill from Gross-Lobke
in the district of Hildesheim,
built in 1812;
dismantled in 1978 and re-erected in 1979 – 81

Unlike tower mills, which first appeared in the 16th century, and somewhat later still in Westphalia, post mills are thought to have been in existence as long ago as the 12th century. Whereas tower millls normally had two or more sets of millstones, the smaller post mills only had one. Up to the first decades of the 19th century, postmills were predominant. By the middle of the 19th century – and much earlier than that in some regions – only the more efficient tower mills were being built. However, we must not overlook the fact that in North Germany there were more watermills than windmills. An inventory compiled in 1819 records a total of 64 watermills, 3 post mills, 41 tower mills and 13 horse-powered mills in the area around Minden.

A victim of the inexorable process of secularization, the prince-bishopric of Hildesheim fell to Prussia in 1803. Shortly afterwards, the Prussian government abolished the so-called 'mill soke'. Up until then the right to build or operate a mill was the exclusive preserve of the local prince, and the people under his jurisdiction were obliged to have their corn milled by him. Following the occupation by French troops – in 1807 Hildesheim was annexed to the Napoleonic Kingdom of Westphalia – freedom of trade was introduced. This resulted in the construction of a large number of windmills under licence. In 1812 Theodor Pape, a local miller, was granted permission to build a post mill on the outskirts of Gross-Lobke. He offered the local community 1,169 francs for the plot of land even though it was officially estimated to be worth only 292.20 francs. Such a generous offer was obviously intended to silence the objections of neighbouring mill owners.

The body or 'buck' of the post mill rests on a single vertical post known as a 'pintle' which is held in position by four diagonal quarter bars secured to a pair of oak cross-trees. The entire body of the mill is turned into the wind by means of a tail-pole which projects from the rear of the buck. The whole structure ist supported on a base of large sandstone plinths, one of which bears the names of subsequent owners of the mill:

H. Pape   L. Pape
geb. Bethmann
1852

These same names appear again on one of the ground-sills:

H Pape   L Pape   geb. B.
1880 gebr.   Huhle

The post mill from Gross-Lobke with its sails fully extended. In the background is the Paderborn village.

The date 1812 is engraved on one of the quarter bars, whilst the tail-pole bears the inscription **H. P. L. P. 1874 A. H.**, denoting the date of its renovation.

The front face of the planked buck ist covered with thousands of oak shingles which provide additional protection against the weather. The mill is divided into two storeys. the uppermost one being the stone floor and the other the bin floor, which is served by a steep external staircase. The internal timbers show elaborate profiles, and are typical of the workmanship of the millwright Heinrich Christian Baars: His name, together with those of the owners, is ornately inscribed on the 'crown-tree', the horizontal beam on which the weight of the buck is supported:

M Theodor Christoph Pape
Johanne Dorothee Borchers
M: Heinrich Christian Baars: 1812 d: 11. Juli

The sails transfer the wind-power to the windshaft on which is mounted a huge brake wheel whose wooden cogs mesh with the wallower. This in turn rotates the stone spindle and with it the higher of the two millstones. Using a hoist at the rear of the mill, the miller winches the sacks of corn on to the stone floor where they are weighed befor being emptied into the hopper. As well as driving the higher of the two millstones, the stone spindle also vibrates the 'damsel' which is situated below the hopper and this ensures that the corn is fed slowly between the millstones. The meal eventually trickles down through a square wooden meal spout either into a sack or into a stifter on the bin floor where it is sieved according to different grades. Although many facets of the milling process were made considerably easier thanks to wind-power, levers and hoists, the miller's work was still very exacting. During the milling operation itself he would constantly be climbing back and forth from one floor to the other, either to add more grain to the hopper, slow down the milling process, change the sacks on the meal spout or check the grade of fineness of the flour and if necessary haul back up the meal which was still too coarse with the sack hoist. And if the sails were rotating too quickly he had to apply the brake.

In addition, the mill hat to be regularly maintained and all its moving parts smeared with grease. Once or even twice a year the grooves in the stones hat to be re-cut. Before he could do this, the miller hat to remove the wooden 'tun' or casing from around the stones and, using the wooden lifting crane which is firmly anchored alongside, had to raise the upper stone and set it down again to one side. So even though there might be no wind there were still plenty of jobs to be done around the mill.

Both of the windmills in the museum have been operated, again since 1980 by a miller permanently employed in the museum.

The post mill being re-erected: 1. the 'pintle', 2. Adding a side wall, 3. Setting the windshaft and brake wheel in position, 4. Putting on the roof.

E 6 – 7 Double watermill plant

The windmiller was largely dependent upon his driving force, the wind, where-as the water miller could determine his working hours rather independently, if only he was in a position to keep sufficient quantities of water in a dammed reservoir. This is why water mills were found wherever water was permanently available, not only to grind corn, but also to drive many other mechanical facilities.

Whether a watermill is operated by an overshot or undershot wheel depends on the quantity and flow speed of the water available. If the running water is strong enough to drive a water wheel, it is undershot, i.e. the water passes underneath the wheel to move it. The overshot alternative makes additional use of the weight of the water falling down on the wheel from a headrace, causing the wheel to turn in the opposite sense. The double watermill plant of the open air museum comprises the backwater pond, the weir, the pothole and the millpond. The slope is rather steep and the protruding waterwheels are driven by an overshot (height of the dam 5.50 m, falling height of the dumping water 4.20 m). The mill is in permanent operation for demonstration purposes (the best way to keep the wheels and building intact).

The Heller watermill which has already been re-erected comprises a set of mill stones to grind corn, and a flax beater equipped with large wooden stampers and a straw cutter connected on the upper floor for simultaneous operation. The second water mill planned opposite the first will be installed for oil pressing and woodworking (saw mill and reciprocating saw).

E 6 Heinrich Heller watermill

Melle-Barkhausen,
rural district of Osnabrück,
built in 1731/1841;
dismantled in 1971, re-erected in 1983 – 84

Up to the beginning of the 19th century, the Heller farm was one of six farms – under unrestricted heritage – of the Barkhausen peasantry belonging to the parish of Buer under the administration of Grönenberg/Osnabrück. At the rise lof the 20th century, the farm covered 37 hectares of land. Under the sovereign leasehold, Heller was awarded with the so called mill prerogative, i.e. permission to run a mill as a secondary trade, and in 1731 this permission was extended to two mills. In the 19th century, the mill which is now in the open air museum was tenanted and was an additional but rather scarce source of income. The mill was closed as early as in 1938.

The re-erected millhouse rests on a ground surface of 7.65 × 9.70 m. Dendonchronological investigation traces it back to 1841 – the archives do not provide any clear evidence of the actual year. A number of wooden parts of 1731 were used for its construction. 1731 is the year in which a previous mill was built on the premises.

The Heller watermill, backwater pond and weir

Whilst in 1812, the Heller mill (previous building) was recorded as having two different mills driven by two overshot headraces, i.e. the set of grinding stones and the flax beater, only one was recorded to serve the two functions in 1868.

The one floor millhouse in its plain half timbered construction resting on a wooden sill, with its front gable half hipped stands immediately at the street which leads over the dam, exactly as it stood on its original site. The grinding stones are at the front, the flax beater is at the back and has an entrance of its own in the right hand eaves wall. The two milling areas are separated by a boarded partition. On the rear threshing floor which is slightly lower still, we find a diesel engine which was used for alternative power since the beginning of the century. This is the time when the mill was completely restored and equipped.

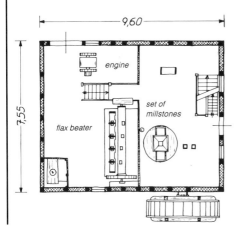

H 1 – 7 Farm from the western Hellweg

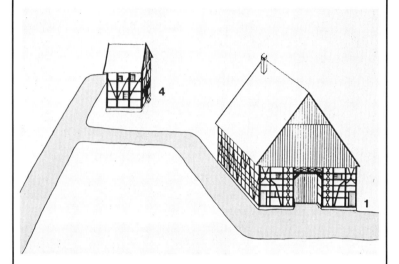

The area of the western Hellweg is essentially the tract of land between the rivers Ruhr and Lippe which we know today as the "Ruhrgebiet", and is flanked in the east by the Soester Börde. It included part of the county of Mark, Vest Recklinghausen and the free imperial town of Dortmund. Apart from a few isolated farmsteads, most of the farms in the Lippe basin occurred in clusters, whilst those in the Ruhr valley were concentrated in small villages. The "Hell-weg", which gave this region its name, was one of the most important east-west trade routes in Europe in the Middle Ages. Side by side with the older, more traditional methods of construction from the Netherlands and the Lower Rhine are the more modern structures from Paderborn and the Weser basin.

The small farmstead in the Museum was largely modelled on a farm from just outside Herne, i.e. as to the number and size of the buildings, the distances between the buildings, and the arrangement and functions of same. With its school and fire station, both of which come from the neighbouring Soester Börde, it forms a kind of focal point for the rural community.

H 1 Farmhouse

from the Segering/Hidding farm
in Dortmund-Brackel, municipality of Dortmund
built in 1793,
dismantled in 1974 and reconstructed in 1978 – 79

This small but magnificent farmhouse was commissioned in 1793 by Johann Diedrich Segering, the eldest son of Johann Heinrich Segering, who was then seventy-five years old. The previous year he had married Katharina Elizabeth Schulte, a farmer's daughter from the neighbouring village of Altenderne. Both their names appear on the arch above the main door. The golden years in the farm's history were probably those around 1790. In 1770 the size of the farm increased by 1.5 hectares to almost 12.5 hectares due to the acquisition of a piece of common land, all of which was being sold off to private buyers.

The early history of the farm is extremely colourful, which is not really surprising given its situation at the crossroads of one of the most important trade routes in central Europe. Built on land belonging to the imperial estate of Brackel of carolingian origin in the 14th century, the Segering farm had a finite lease which was held by the church in Brackel. It had to be renewed every 15 years. In the 18th century the farm experienced frequent crises which almost invariably led to a reduction in the ground rent. In 1761 and 1762, during the Seven Years War, the entire harvest was confiscated by the French. Rent arrears, unpaid debts, bad harvests, hail storms and damage through mice were recurrent themes in the years 1772, 1777, 1788 and 1789. It must be said, however, that only the disastrous years were ever recorded, little or no reference being made in the registers to the years of plenty. In 1837 the fixed-term lease, which cost 10 taler every 15 years, was converted into an inheritable tenancy for a fee of 50 taler, and in 1871 the farm was bought form the church in Brackel for a sum of 5,000 marks.

In 1848 Carl Johann Caspar Dietrich Wilhelm Hidding, the son of a neighbouring family, married the owner of the farm, Johanna Klara Haarbrink, who went under the name of Segering. In accordance with local custom, Karl, too had to adopt the name of the estate, i.e. Segering. Under Karl Hidding the farm gradually reduced in size. In 1847 he was obliged to sell land to accommodate the Cologne-Minden railway. In 1926 further stretches of land were expropriated to enable the building of Dortmund airport. The remaining 5.25 hectares were leased to neighbouring farms. This was the end of the agricultural operations.

Like all new buildings erected in the Hellweg region during the 18th century, this house has very high walls and consists of a central nave and two side aisles, all having the same height. Also typical of this region are the rhythmical combinations of angle braces which adorn the outer walls and whose function is more decorative than structural. In the course of the 19th century the thatched roof was replaced with a covering of blue-grey pantiles and the previously bare timberwork received a coat of black paint. The window frames, on the other hand, have always been white.

View from the rear of the Hellweg farm showing Senner horses in the paddock

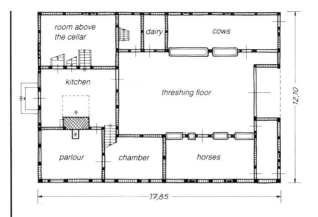

The porchway in the front gable is surrounded on either side by a vertical row of St. Andrew's crosses. A number of religious maxims are engraved on the lintel over the door:

JOHAN DIDERRICH SIERING   ANNA CATRINA
ESEBET SCHULTEN VON ALTENDEREN / WO GOT
ZUM HAUS NICHT GIBT SEIN GVNS ARBEITET
JEDERMANN UMSONS   WO GOT DIS HUS NICHT
SELBST BEWACHT SO IS UMSONS DER WAHR
WACHT / BEWAHRE GOT DIS HAUS FUR WASSER
UND FEERSNOT   JESUS WON IN DISEM HAUS /
WEICHE NIMER MER DARAUS
DEN 11 JULLIUS   ANO 1793

The Segering farmhouse in 1935

The owners of the farm, Hidding called Segering
(wedding 1848)   *Photograph taken prior to 1882*

The threshing floor forms a self-contained unit since both of the side aisles have been partitioned off. The wider left-hand aisle houses a stable and hamees room, whilst the one on the right contains a number of cow stalls, above which is a cereal loft. A wooden platform on which corn was stored is suspended above the narrow dairy and the adjoining store room. The striking pebble-stone laid in a herring bone pattern floor was almost certainly included when the house was built.

At the far end of the building, the living quarters, which are separated off completely from the working area, provide clear evidence of the changing face of domestic life at the end of the 19th century. This whole area, including the kitchen space, is divided into two storeys, each comprising a number of different rooms. Unlike those in older houses, the kitchen, which has an   79 exceptionally low ceiling, does not extend from one eaves wall to the other or give on to a suite of chambers at its rear, but is situated in the middle of the living area and is reached by a door in the rear gable. This arrangement is typical of small farms in the Hellweg region. The original fireplace no longer exists and has been replaced with one of similar design from the Fronden farm in Fröndenberg-Warmen in the district of Unna. Its hood, which is attached to the kitchen ceiling, could not possibly have removed all the smoke given off by the fire, and this is why part of the space above the kitchen houses a further canopy and a smoke-bay.

The kitchen provides access to all the other rooms. The three doors in the right-hand wall lead to two narrow storage cellars and to the chamber directly above them; the first of the two doors to the right of the fireplace leads into the parlour and its adjoining chamber, whilst the other conceals a flight of stairs which leads up to the rooms set aside for the retired members of the family. The contract signed by Carl Johann Caspar Dietrich Wilhelm Hidding (called Segering) in 1882 transferring the ownership of the farm to his third son Johann Wilhelm, who was born in 1857, does not specify which particular rooms in the house were to be put at the disposal of the retiring couple. It merely states that *„the son, Dietrich, undertakes to provide for his parents accommodation befitting their status and appropriate to their needs for as long as may be required ... and in particular to set aside two rooms of their choosing, one for living in and one for sleeping in, for their exclusive use".* He was also obliged to provide them with furniture, clothing, lighting, heating, food and drink, as well as paying them an annual rent of 150 taler, which was a considerable sum for a small farm such as this.

H 2 Gatehouse

Neuhoff farm,
Dortmund-Eichlinghofen, municipality of Dortmund,
built around 1704,
dismantled in 1985, re-erected in 1986 – 87

The Neuhoff farm, recorded since approximately 1400, was owned by noble families of the Mark, in the 16th century the owners were a family named Rabe von Thulen. From 1595 on, the Neuhoff family lived on the farm as tenants. Between 1705 and 1912, the size of the farm varied from 24 to 29 hectares of land. In 1846, the lease could be terminated by a purchase agreement stating a sum of 4,570 Taler. In the 19th century the farm counted six buildings. The farmhouse, the stable, the shed, the barn, the bakehouse and another dwelling house.

Gatehouse from Eichlinghofen being re-erected 1986

In the 18th century, the barn was constructed as a complete half timbered building. The transversal passage was flanked at its right hand side by a large part of the building which was subdivided for use as a coachhouse and granary, and on the opposite side by a smaller part accommodating various barn bays. That side of the larger part which faces the farmhouse attracts special attention, because it must be understood as an open hall featuring three entrance doors on the ground floor. There are still traces evidencing the different posts. On the upper floor, the actual building had a passage in front, the panels of which were infilled in the parapet only and served as an open fronted portico. About 1800, the ground floor was renewed, and the jettied open fronted portico was completely underpinned with square shaped quarry stones. Since that time the ground floor was no longer used as a coach house, but as a roomy stable. According to a decree passed by the municipality of Dortmund, the barn opposite the gateway had to be taken down in 1968 because of its ruinous condition. It could yet be reconstructed following old photographs and various traces on the woodwork of the gateway.

H 3 Shed

(planned)

H 4 Granary

from the Streil farm in Olfen-Vinnum
in the district of Coesfeld,
built in 1727,
dismantled in 1965 and re-erected in 1978

This granary is a multi-purpose building. The name of the builder, **JODOKUS HUSSER,** is engraved on the lintel above the door on the left. The ground-floor room was used as a shed and workshop, and as a feeding passage for the two stalls over on the right.

The granary itself was on the floor above and at some stage a small space measuring only 60 cm across was partitioned off from the rear gable by a half-timbered wall. This dark hideaway could not be detected either from the inside or the outside and its sole means of access was a loose board in the floor of the loft. During World War II two young Jews hid themselves away here for two whole years.

The most strikting features on the outside of this building, which stands 8.5 metres high, are the unusually long braces between the wall posts.

Workshop on the ground floor of the granary

H 5 Fire Station

from Welver-Einecke
in the district of Soest,
built in 1846,
dismantled in 1971 and re-erected in 1980

*The fire station
before being
dismantled in 1971*

Im Jahr 1846 d. 23 t. Mai Hatt die Gemeinde Eineke dieses
Gebäide . . . erbauth

The name of the carpenter who constructed this building,
which is engraved above the door arch, is barely legible.
According to the local records, he was called Andreas Kerstin,
and in 1846 he was put in charge of the fire station.
The piece of land on which it was built was made available free
of charge by a man called Colon Hohoff, who was head of the
local assembly. Its useful life came to an end in 1971 when the
newly established district of Welver built a central fire station
designed to serve all the towns and villages within its pre-
cincts. The manually operated water-pump, which was made in
1911 and later mechanised, the ladders and some of the
leather buckets formed part of the original inventory. In the far
left-hand corner is a small detention-cell where miscreants
were held before being escorted away by the local policeman.

H 6 School

from the village of Thöningsen
in the district of Soest,
built in 1837,
dismantled in 1970 and re-erected in 1982

The municipality of Thöningsen in the Soester Börde comprised the small villages of Thöningsen, Lühringsen and Kutmecke, which in the 19th century had a combined population of between 150 and 200 spread across 30 households. 20 of these were farmsteads with an average of 25 – 50 hectares of land. The village of Thöningsen belonged to the parish of Wiese-Georg in Soest. Thus, when compulsory education was introduced in 1763 the children ought to have gone to school in Soest. However, presumably in order to spare them the 5-kilometer walk, they were taught by the village tailor, Holtmann, in his own home. In 1818 the communities of Thöningsen and Balksen founded a school association which built its own school in 1837.

The school is a simple timber-framed building mounted on a quarry-stone base. The only door opens on to a small lobby which served as a draught screen and a cloakroom. The classroom itself measures only 5.90 × 5.30 metres and was supposed to accommodate as many as 50 children at a time. The most important fixtures and fittings are the teacher's desk, the rows of benches, a cylindrical stove and the teaching material on the walls. The oil-impregnated floor was cleaned once a week.

However, the children of school age from the two small communities never added up to 50. The number attending the school at anyone time varied between 10 and 40, and they continued to be taught in two separate groups until 1870: those under the age of 10, between 7 and 10 a. m. and the older ones from noon until 3 p. m. The original curriculum included religious education, reading and writing, mathematics, geography and history. Physical train-

Classroom furnished and decorated with teaching materials

Photograph of a school form to Thöningsen 1910

ing was introduced around 1860.

Although compulsory, attendance was not always regular to begin with. Despite the fact that fines could be imposed for non-attendance: the tending of cattle and bad weather kept many children away. By 1889, only 6 of the remaining 16 children still had more than a thirty minutes walk to school. But by then classes had been extended to two sessions per day, which meant a total journey-time in excess of two hours. Only four of the children lived in Thöningsen itself.

Unlike the very first village teacher, Holtmann the tailor, whose only formal training had been in his own trade, those who succeeded him were trained at the college of education in Soest, which was founded in 1805. One of them was Florenz Pape, the farmer's son from Thöningsen, during whose period in office (1814–1870) the new school was built. Writing in 1908, the District Inspector of Schools complained that: *"The classroom is in a building which bears a closer resemblance to a stable than a school."* This one-room school was eventually closed in 1964. Since then the children have been attending the central school in Bad Sassendorf.

H 7 Apiary

from the Neuhoff farm,
Dortmund-Eichlinghofen, municipality of Dortmund,
built in 1880/81;
dismantled in 1985, re-erected in 1987

The small apiary which leant to a sturdy garden wall in Eichlinghofen is faced with thin planklike braces securing the beehives against theft, and giving the bees the space required for their entrances and exits. When the apiary was built in 1880/1881, the wooden frame of an earlier apiary of the early 19th century may have been incorporated. Bees were only kept until about 1925.

J 1 – 10 Farm from Westmünsterland

The western region of the Münsterland once formed part of the prince-bishop-ric of Münster and was cut off from central Münsterland by stretches of heath and moorland. It borders the Lower Rhine and the Netherlands and has been strongly influenced by their respective cultures throughout its history. The region is characterised not by villages but by scattered settlements consisting of thousands of isolated farmsteads. And because the soil is so sandy, most of them are pastoral.

The farmhouses in West Münsterland fall into the category of North German "hall-houses", although in terms of their appearance and construction they differ considerably from hall-houses to be found elsewhere. Their wooden frames are not closely woven grids composed of powerful squared timbers, but are wide-meshed structures made from oak scantling. Another distinguish-ing feature of these buildings is the so-called "anchor-beam" method of con-struction, in which each pair of opposing wall posts, set at right angles to the axis of the house, is secured to a horizontal beam by means of mortise and tenon joints which are normally situated about 50 – 100 cm below the crown of each post. The tenoned ends of the beam protrude quite a way beyond the front face of the wall post where they are held in position with wooden pegs. Thus jointed, the posts and beams form a frame. When the building is being assembled the frames are erected one after the other and are locked into posi-tion by the wall plates.

The wall posts are not mounted on ground sills but on individual piers of sand-stone or brick. The external walls are frequently supported on a base of large sandstone blocks of wall thickness, called plinths. A series of angle braces between the posts and the wall platers lend additional stability to the building, reaching from the posts to the headrail.

The external appearance of these structures is extremely modest. The use of pantiles for roofs and brick for infilling the timber framework increased con-siderably after the 16th century. The weatherboarding which covers the gable pediments is unusually deep and generally extends below the level of the loft. Due to the nature of their construction, very few of the buildings carry inscriptions.

The farm in the museum is a faithful re-creation of a typical middle-sized pastoral farm from west Münsterland as it would have looked in the late 18th century. In addition to the house and the various outbuildings dotted around the farmyard, there is also a symmetrically arranged Late-Baroque garden, which is enclosed by a hornbeam hedge; an oak tree plantation; several dyke hedges; and a number of adjoining fields. Next to the well, which was sunk in 1756 (the curb dates from 1859) a revolving cartwheel on which the crockery was stood to dry.

J 1 Farmhouse

from the Resing farm
in Borken-Rhedebrügge in the district of Borken,
built in 1790;
dismantled in 1963 and re-erected between 1973 – 76

The Resing farm is known to have belonged to the Benedictine monastery in Abdinghof near Paderborn as long ago as the 13th century. In the 16th century it was acquired as a fief by the lord of Rhede Castle, who sold part of it in 1575 and the remainder in 1598 to the Hospital of the Holy Spirit in Borken. The rights of the monastery were not affected in any way by this sale.

The farm remained a leasehold property until its sale in 1962. The lease had to be renewed every twelve years. This legal relationship did not, however, prevent the property from being handed down from father to son, and families

Westmünsterland farm

were not evicted even when they committed gross breaches of the terms of the lease. The Hospital of the Holy Spirit in Borken used the considerable revenues which accrued from this and other farms to care for the poor in the town. Every year the tenant paid taxes, both in money and in kind. In addition, he was obliged to plant a certain number of trees and to make himself as well as his draught cattle, gears and harness available for work and carriage Services on the owner's estate, as required. Every twelve years he had to pay a form of profit tax.

The amount of land attached to the farm fluctuated between 12.5 and 25 hectares from one century to the next, whilst the number of people (including servants) varied between four and ten.

The layout of the house remains as it was at the time of building. To the left of the threshing floor are the cow stalls, adjoining which is a modest sleeping chamber containing a box-bed. In the opposite aisle the small stable next to the cow and calf stalls is indicative of the lack of importance attached to arable farming on this predominantly pastoral farm. The blue limewash on all the walls was a common sight throughout west Münsterland for several decades, and this is borne out by the number of coats which have obviously been applied to this building.

At the far end of the building, and separated from the threshing floor by a wall, is the kitchen, whose furnishings and decor date from around 1860. There are clear signs here of the cultural influences assimilated from neighbouring regions: the transom windows, which are sash-like in appearance, the tiles on the rear gable wall and around the fireplace, the tin-glazed earthenware (delftware), oval drop-leaf tables, the shild's heated box-seat, which kept out draughts, are all cultural imports

View of the gable at the "living end" of the Resing farmhouse   *1935*

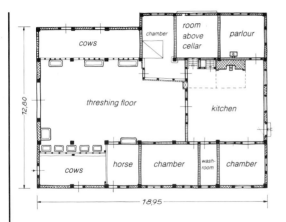

from the Netherlands. The cabinets and cupboards, on the other hand, drew their inspiration from the Lower Rhine.

The kitchen floor, which bears the date 1847, and the two-tone circular cross at its centre are composed of small quarry-stone blocks, whilst the peg-top paving around the fireplace and in the wash-room consists of strips of stoneware made in the local potters' villages of Vreden and Stadtlohn.

The living rooms are not situated behind the kitchen, but on either side of it. On the left, next to the "Upkamer", the room above the storage cellar, is the so-called "warm chamber" or parlour. The right hand aisle, meanwhile, houses the parental bedroom, the wash-room and the weaving room, the latter being the only room in the house with a clay floor.

The Resing farmhouse, view from the farmyard

Craftsmen at the Open Air Museum re-laying the kitchen floor
from 1847 in the Resing farmhouse. Occasionally it was possible
for whole sections to be transferred intact 1975

Several of the pictures on the walls, the baroque crucifix on the chimney breast, the souvenirs of past pilgrimages in the parlour and the decorative cross at the apex of the rear gable are all indicative of the fact that west Münsterland was a bastion of Catholicism.

The kitchen and fireplace in the Resing farmhouse

The door and almost all the windows and shutters in the front gable wall date from 1790 when the house was built. A sandstone plaque situated between the kitchen windows carries the following inscription:

IOHAN HENDRICK · RES:/ING · VND · IANMA ·/ RGRIETA · RIDDER · HA/BEN · GEBAVT · DIESES/ HAVSZ · GOTT · WE ·/NDE · ALL · VNGLÜCK/ DAR · AVS/DEN · 21. IVNIVS/ANNO · 1790.

A further date appears again on a row of commemorative bricks immediately above the brick ground sill on the left-hand eaves wall. The names of the members of the Rider and Resing families who helped make the clamp-fired bricks which were used for infilling the panels of the timber frame, together with that of the brickmaker himself, are immortalised here, too, between the sign of the cross and the date when the bricks were fired, each having a stone bearing his or her initials:

IHS / IGR / IHR / IMGR / GALR / IR / IWR / JAR / JBR / AGDR / IGNH / ANO / 1789

The date 1789 indicates that the bricks were made the year before the so-called "topping-out" ceremony, which took place in June 1790 and was a celebration to mark the erection of the roof timbers.

The well from 1756 and the quart-wheel for drying crockery

The two post and beam frame being dismantled   1975

J 2 Barn

from the Siehoff-Bensing farm
in Vreden-Ellewick in the district of Borken,
built around 1775,
dismantled in 1975 and re-erected in 1976

With its sweeping pantile roof and weatherboarding on all four walls, this aisled barn is almost tent-like in appearance. Like those of sheepfolds, the double doors below the deep covering of weatherboarding on the jettied gable pediment open outwards and have retained their original wooden hinges. From the inside the wide spacing of the timbers so characteristic of the "anchor beam" method of construction is clearly visible; in all, the building comprises six "frames" spaced at intervals of more than 250 cm. Whereas both side aisles are open to the rafters, the central aisle is covered over, one half with fixed wooden boards, the other with slender cylindrical poles which could be removed if necessary. The barn was used for storing hay and straw, most of it being stacked on the bare floor, the remainder up on the boards and poles.
Outbuildings of this type and appearance were common throughout west Münsterland, where they served as wagon sheds, wood stores, sheepfolds or barns, some of which even had a threshing floor or a distilling room.
In addition to housing hay and straw, this particular barn was also used as a store for firewood, as well as serving from time to time as a sheepfold. The first bay in the left-hand aisle was at some point converted into a stable.

J 3 Wagon shed

from the Stening-Böving farm
in Schöppingen-Tinge in the district of Borken,
built in 1743,
dismantled in 1966 and re-erected in 1975

For most of the year the main body of this building, which is open on three sides, served as a wagon shed and a general storage area. Hay was kept in the roof space above the through-passage and was loaded and unloaded through a small pitching-hole in the eaves facing the farmyard. That side of the building away from the farmyard once had even less headroom than it has now. It was altered in the 19th century so that it could be turned into animal stalls. The long diagonal braces which adorn the wall facing the farmyard are an unusual feature even for west Münsterland. Particularly striking are the pegged tenons associated with the "anchor beam" method of construction which project from each of the principal posts. Two of these posts carry inscriptions giving the date of construction and the names of the original owner and the carpenter:

A N N O	DEN 8
1 7 4 3	JULIU
I : B :	M :G:L E
	M :I:K

The wagon shed from Tinge

J 4 Bakehouse

from the Lammerding farm
in Gescher-Büren in the district of Borken,
built in 1747,
dismantled and re-erected in 1974

This small building, which has a floor area of 6.6 × 6 metres, is situated at a similar distance from the farmhouse in the Museum as it was on the Lammerding farm. Although the baking oven was missing at the time of dismantling, in all other respects the building was in exceptionally good condition and had not been altered in any way, making it one of the few structures in the Museum in which practically nothing needed to be replaced.

Whilst almost every small farm in Westphalia had a bakehouse, only the larger ones had installations for distilling "schnaps" and brewing beer. In west Münsterland, however, such installations were much more common. The distilling or brewing equipment might well have been housed in a granary, a shed, a barn or, as in this case, in a bakehouse. Very occasionally, separate buildings were erected exclusively for this purpose.

The bakehouse on the Lammerding farm   *1974*

In addition to the baking and brewing parlour, the bakehouse from Gescher-Büren also contains a shallow beer cellar with a vaulted brick ceiling. Unfortunately, the baking oven and some of the brewing: equipment have never been found.

Particularly striking are the diagonal courses of brick which have been inlaid over the slender angle braces in the eaves walls. In the middle of the front gable wall is the only decorative infilling on the entire farm. Unusually, it is possible to make out the inscription on the wide lintel above the door. It begins by invoking the Virgin Mary, Jesus and Joseph and ends with the initials of the original owner and the date of construction:

MAR   IHS   IOS
JE LANGER IE MER KER DICh ZV GOT
DAS DV NICHt WIRSt DES TEVffELS SPOtt
ES KRICht DER MENSch EIN SOLchEN LOhN
WIE ER IM LEBEN hat GEDhAN
B.L.I.N.MA.LH. EL.AO. 1747 D 24 OCt

J 5 Clay-coated granary

from the Scholten farm
in Neuhaus-Grasdorf,
in the district of Grafschaft Bentheim,
built in 1454,
dismantled in 1965 and re-erected in 1974

The clay-coated granary from the Scholten Farm is currently the oldest building in the Open Air Museum. Although it has a floor area of only 4.46 × 4.75 metres, it towers almost 9.25 metres above the small man-made island on which it is perched. Both the function and structure of this building are rooted firmly in the tradition of the Middle Ages. All four outer walls were once completely covered with clay, which provided the corn, seed and other crops inside with excellent protection against fire. In times of crisis the granary would probably have served as a refuge for the farmer and his family as well as a safe haven for their valuables. The surrounding moat, which was uncovered during the course of excavation work at its former site, is further proof of the defensive role of this building. The wooden planks which form the light footbridge over the moat were discovered at the same time. In the museum the outer coating of clay has been omitted from two of the walls in order to give the visitor an insight into the methods of construction which prevailed in the late Middle Ages. Each wall is crossed with a single pair of intersecting braces which run diagonally between the corner posts. They are nothing more than thin strips of wood which are merely laid across the structural timbers and secured to them with wooden nails.

This so-called "scissor bracing", using halved and lapped laths of timber, first appeared in towns during the Middle Ages in the period of transition from single- to multi-storey timber-framed buildings.

The clay-coated granary from Grasdorf. The outer clay shell has been omitted from two of the walls to provide an insight into the method of construction. The other two sides have been restored to their original condition.

J 6 Bleaching hut

(planned)

J 7 Corn granary

from the Meyer farm
in Havixbeck-Lasbeck in the district of Coesfeld,
built in 1820,
dismantled in 1966 and re-erected in 1974 − 75

Farmers in the Baumbergen region used to refer to these buildings as "Spieker up Musepile" or "granaries on mouse piers". This one-room timber-framed building, three partitions deep, is a perfect square measuring 6.80 × 6.80 metres, and has a total height of 7.80 metres. It rests on a series of small sandstone staddles whose primary purpose − as indeed their colloquial name suggests − was to prevent the corn from being ravaged by mice. They also facilitated good ventilation. As in almost all granaries to be found in North Germany, the corn was not kept in special containers but was stored in loose mounds on the wooden floor.

J 8 Oat barn

from the Schulze-Weddeling farm
in Velen-Holthausen, in the district of Borken,
built in 19th century,
dismantled and re-erected in 1975

97

Barns supported on staddle-stones were a very common sight throughout West Münsterland during the 18th and 19th centuries. They were usually covered with weatherboarding and were generally somewhat taller than the example in the Museum. They were used for storing hay or cereals which were loaded and unloaded through pitching-holes in the wall rather than through doors.

This barn from the Schulze-Weddeling Farm was built in the 19th century. The stone staddle substructure carries a brick plinth serving as a base for the timber frame of a small three aisled barn built in the 18th century, the aisles of which were not added again. The external walls are partly infilled with brick and partly weatherboarded.

J 9 Flax oven

from the Thesseling farm
in Stadtlohn-Hengeler in the district of Borken,
built around 1860,
dismantled and re-erected in 1974

Next to wool, flax was the principal material used in textile making. The process of turning flax into linen was a lengthy one involving a number of different stages: sowing, reaping, rippling, bleaching, retting, braking, hackling, spinning and, finally, weaving. After being left to soak for several days in a pond, some farmers of the Western Münsterland let the flax dry in a purpose-built oven. This allowed the fibres to be separated more easily from the stalks.

On the Thesseling farm, as in the museum, the flax oven was sited well away
from the farmyard to prevent the fire from spreading   *1974*

The flax oven from the Thessling Farm has two vaults made from clamp-fired bricks. It was heated in the same way as a baking oven, and after the embers and ashes had been removed the flax was placed in the vaults and left to dry. Because they constituted a fire hazard, flax ovens were always sited well away from the farmyard.

J 10 Covered haystack

from the Brummelhuis farm
in Bentfeld in the province of Delden, Netherlands,
built around 1900,
dismantled in 1976 and re-erected in 1978

It was still possible to find isolated examples of this type of covered haystacks in the Münsterland until the middle of this century. They originally came from the Netherlands and were used for storing hay which was either stacked on the ground or suspended slightly above it on a hurdle, when there was no more space left in the house. The adjustable roof, which provided protection against the weather, allowed variable amounts of fodder to be stored. Because they were little more than wooden posts embedded in the ground, such structures did not normally have a very long life expectancy.

The covered haystack being dismantled in 1976

K 1 – 13 Moated farmstead from Central Münsterland

Central Münsterland comprises the large tract of land around Münster, which was once the principal town of the local prince-bishopric and later became a prussian provincial centre. It includes the city of Münster itself, the district of Warendorf, as well as parts of the neighbouring districts of Coesfeld, Steinfurt and Gütersloh.

During the Middle Ages moated farms served as lightly fortified places of passive defence. The farms which were protected in this way were principally those inhabited by members of the nobility in the service of the king. There were several hundred moated farms altogether, some of them with as much as 375 hectares of land which passed undivided from one generation to the next.

Like those in the west of the region, the buildings in Central Münsterland – an area which is similarly characterised by scattered and isolated farmsteads – are very simple in appearance: Their timberwork is unpainted, their gables weatherboarded, their walls infilled with brick and their roofs are covered with pantiles.

The moated farmstead in the Museum extends across four small islands which respectively accommodate the farmhouse and a number of outbuildings, the barn, the granary and the garden. The one on which the house stands is shaped like a fried egg and has a gatehouse at its tip. The granary is reached by a footbridge, whilst access to the garden is provided by a drawbridge. There is a sundial dating from 1711 in the central flowerbed of this Baroque garden, which is enclosed by a box-hedge. The farm has been recreated to look as it would have done around 1800, by which time its moat was already partly grassed over.

View from the rear of the moated farm from Schulte-Bisping   *1966*

The timber frame of the house from the Schulte-Bisping farm being reconstructed in 1968

K 1 Farmhouse

from the Schulte-Bisping farm
in Albersloh-Alst in the district of Warendorf,
built in 1787,
dismantled in 1967 and re-erected in 1967 – 69

This house was originally attached to a manor farm which presided over 133 hectares of land, some of it acquired as a result of the selling of common land to private buyers in the early 19th century. It is a magnificent aisled building measuring $42 \times 15 \times 15$ metres, and was built in 1787 to replace the original house which was destroyed by fire. The owners of the property, the chapter of Münster cathedral, insisted that the new house should measure at least 140 feet long and 50 feet wide. The name of the farm, Bisping (literally "man of the bishop"), is indicative of the allegiance owed to the Church by the tenant.

The names of the original occupants are displayed on the arch above the door, either side of the monogram of Christ:

EVERHARDT HENRICH   VND ANNA CATNARINA
SCHVLTE BISPINK   IHS   BVSCHKAMP EHELVTE
ANNO 1787   DEN 15 JVNIVS

The arrangement of the rooms in this building must have seemed exceptionally advanced at the time, because in 1790, three years after it was built, a similar "model" floor plan – not for a manor house, but for a middle-sized farmhouse – was published by Anton Bruchhausen in his book *"Anweisungen zur Verbesserung des Ackerbaues und der Landwirthschaft des Münsterlandes".*

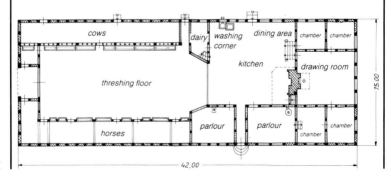

102

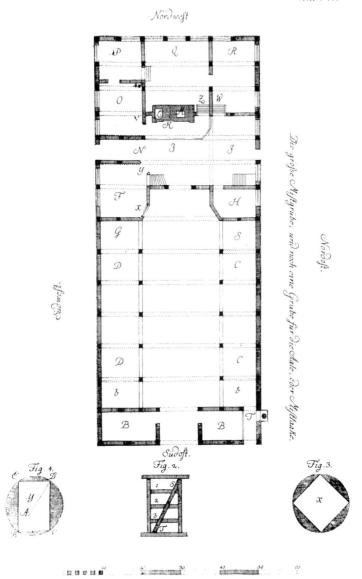

Floor plan for a Münsterland farmhouse published by Anton Bruchhausen in 1790

The kitchen in the Schulte-Bisping farmhouse

The building is entered through an opening recessed to shelter the doorway from the weather. The threshing floor, flanked on either side by stalls in which calves and geese were kept, has a covering of sandstone flags from Baumberg, some of them more than 2 metres square. The twenty or so cows and bullocks which occupied the deep-litter stalls on the left and the horses — between ten and twelve of them in all — which were stabled in the wide aisle on the right were fed from here. An inventory compiled in 1628 records the number of animals kept in the previous house: There were 12 horses, four milk cows and 13 bullocks. In contrast, the records show that in 1754 there were 8 horses, 2 oxen, 6 dairy cows and 31 beef cattle. The large number of horses is indicative both of the economic importance of the farm and of the amount of land under cultivation. The loft space above the stalls was used for storing fodder and threshed straw.

A huge panelled door, which remained open throughout the summer, separates the threshing floor from the kitchen („Flett"), the main living room. In winter, access from the one area to the other was provided by a small side door. Only a few years before this house was built a partition wall between the working and living ends would have been unthinkable. The door acts as a kind of wind-break, moderating the through-draught produced by the chimney. The handsome fireplace was both the main source of heat and the only means of cooking in the house. The fire-surround, which dates from 1707, is decorated with scenes from the Old Testament (Jacob at the well, Adam and Eve). It ensured that the heat from the fire was

Gable of the farmhouse, bakehouse and old granary, view from the garden island.

reflected out into the kitchen, whilst an ‚air furnace' made of sandstone kept the cooked food warm.

The hood over the fireplace and the rows of rods which lined the ceiling were used for curing and keeping sausages, bacon and ham. The ham produced here was famous throughout the region and beyond, and probably explains why the place became known as ‚The Paradise of Westphalia'.

On the left of the kitchen-cum-living area are the washing corner with its sink and the dining area, where both family and servants took their meals. The glass cabinet in the dining area is more than 3 metres tall and serves as a showcase for valuable pieces of tableware. The kitchen provides access to all the rooms and chambers in the house. The door next to the washing corner leads through to the dairy, above which are the maids' sleeping quarters. The male farm hands slept over the cattle stalls in the two aisles on either side of the porch. Over to the right a narrow passage runs from the kitchen to a door in the side wall. It is the last vestige of the type of kitchen found in older houses in the Münsterland which extended from one eaves wall to the other. The so-called ‚winter parlour' adjoining the passage was heated by a front-loading stove which was only lit on extremely cold winter days. During the summer the room was given over to certain domestic tasks. The elegant room on the other side of the passage, which contains a tapestry embroidered with a French landscape, and the sleeping chamber at its rear were used by the landlord's representative in Münster whenever he came to visit.

Farm house, washing corner in the kitchen

The suite of chambers beyond the fireplace included sleeping quarters for the unmarried members of the family, for the children and for the grandparents. The large drawing-room in the middle served both as the parental bedroom and as a reception room für distinguished visitors. The original fireplace in this room was removed towards the end of the 19th century. It has been replaced with one from the Albers farm in Neuenkirchen which is decorated with religious symbols „arma christi" or instruments of the passion. The canopied bed, which is draped with curtains and the pigeonhole at the headboard comes from north-east Münsterland and is typical of the extremely short beds which were favoured in all rural areas until the mid-19th century (it was obviously customary for people to sleep with their legs tucked closely into their bodies).

The living room, the drawing room and the room containing the tapestry all have stained-glass windows which contain some coats of arms. They are likely to have been donated by good friends of the family to celebrate the completion of the house or perhaps a christening. The names, occupations and places to which they refer bear eloquent testimony to the excellent social connections which the family had established within upper-class circles.

The linen trunk in the aisle leading to the chambers

Stained-glass windows in the farmhouse: The one on the left shows the crest of the Bailiff of Aldrup, whilst the one on the right depicts a scene from a fable.

K 2 Gatehouse

from the Uhlenkotten farm
in Münster-Nienberge, municipality of Münster,
built in 1767,
dismantled in 1967 and re-erected in 1968

Like many castles, a large number of moated farms were only accessible by means of a gatehouse equipped with a drawbridge, which would eventually have been replaced by a fixed bridge.

According to the inscription above the door, this particular gatehouse — also known as a ,keeper's lodge' — with its quarter-hipped roof was built in 1767 by the then ,Meyer auf Uhlenkotten'. The people who lived on this farm were only tenants. It was owned during the 16th and 17th centuries by the well-to-do Grüter family of merchants and aldermen who were residents of the city of Münster.

The six small loopholes in the front wall would seem to suggest that the gatehouse fulfilled a defensive role. In this period, however, they had a decorative rather than a military function. The building is divided into three zones, The middle zone is a paved through-passage, and the one to its left is where the farm vehicles and agricultural implements were kept (old ploughs with wooden mould boards, a machine for sowing root crops, wooden harrows, a land roller, a manure cart, a covered wagon.

The third zone contains a workshop called „Timmerkammer", an important facility on a self-sufficient farm such as this. All the essential maintenance and repair work was carried out here, and quite a few of the more simple wooden implements were made by the farmer himself. There is a band-saw operated by foot pedal and a fairly primitive lathe on which a spinning wheel, for example, might have been fashioned. And of course no workshop would be complete without a carpenter's bench.

Gatehouse from the Uhlenkotten farm

The workshop in the gatehouse

K3 Wood shed

from the Meier Osthoff farm
in Harsewinkel-Beller in the district of Gütersloh,
built around 1860,
dismantled in 1970 and re-erected in 1970 – 71

This shed was designed specifically for storing and drying firewood. The honeycombed brickwork permits a constant through-draught which speeds up the drying process. The relatively slender timbers of this building, the simple diagonal braces which extend from the ground sill to the wall plate, the absence of a projecting upper storey and the spruce weatherboarding which covers the gable pediment all point to a fairly recent construction.

K4 New granary

from the Meier Osthoff farm
in Harsewinkel-Beller in the district of Gütersloh,
built 1711,
dismantled in 1969 and re-erected in 1969 – 70

Wood store, new granary and bakehouse on the moated farm. All three originally came from the Meier Osthoff farm in Harsewinkel.

Until the late 18th century, most of the large farms in the Münsterland, and indeed throughout Westphalia, had purpose-built granaries for storing threshed corn and seed. They were usually two-storey buildings with a small floor area and had doors and hatches on each floor.

This tower-shaped Meier Osthoff granary is situated in close proximity to the kitchen. The principal wall posts, which rise the full height of the building, support the ceiling joists in the upper storey as well as those in the loft. The lavish exterior with its imposing Baroque portal, the double doors with their pretty iron handle, the handsomely carved door-head which bears the family crest, and the bunch of ornamental grapes at the apex of the twice overhanging pediment are all indicative of the high value placed on the contents within. Corn was both the staple food of the household and also a valuable cash crop. This building has the only gable pediment on the entire farm which is not shrouded with weather-boarding. The two pitching-holes situated below the hoist-beam were restored at the beginning of the 19th century in late-classical style. Sacks of corn were hauled in and out with the aid of a powerful hoist in the loft. The inscription over the door reads:

$$AC \dagger W$$
$$AN \cdot NO \cdot \quad M \text{ w } 10 \qquad \cdot 17 \cdot 11 \cdot$$

K 5 Bakehouse

from the Meier Osthoff farm
in Harsewinkel-Beller in the district of Gütersloh,
built in 1695,
dismantled in 1968 and re-erected in 1969 – 70

Most of the scattered and isolated farmsteads in this region had their own bakehouse. Due to the high fire risk which they posed, they were usually sited some distance away from the farmyard. They contained all the equipment necessary for preparing and baking bread, such as a trough for kneading the dough, a bread ladle, a rake for removing the embers and ashes and an implement for cleaning the oven. There were also wooden hurdles on which fruit could be dried. The brick baking vault, which is attached to the rear gable, is coated with a thick layer of clay in order to minimise heat loss.

The bakehouse on the Meier Osthoff Farm does not have a chimney. The smoke would pour from the mouth of the oven into the baking room and out through the barred window above the entrance door. Every two weeks or so the vaulted oven would be stoked with beechwood and left for several hours until it was hot enough for baking. After it had been emptied of its ashes and cleaned, the loaves of leave black bread known as ‚pumpernickel‘, each weighing between 15 and 20 pounds, were placed in the hot oven and left for a good 20 hours. The sweet white bread did not take nearly so long to bake. The surplus heat from the oven was used for drying fruit. The building ca be dated by the richly carved brackets which support the gable pediment.

K 6 Old granary

from the Schulte Brüning farm
in Everswinkel-Wieningen in the district of Warendorf,
built around 1565,
dismantled in 1968 and re-erected in 1969

There are a large number of solid or timber-framed multi-storey granarics scatter-ed throughout the Münsterland, many of which served as places of refuge in times of crisis. They are, or were, almost always built on small islands sur-rounded by a moat. The upper storey contained living quarters complete with leaded glass windows, a washing area, a lavatory and sometimes even a fire-place. To date no research has been done into the origins and development of this type of granary. They are believed to have been built not by the farmers but by the owners of the property (the nobility or the monasteries). There would appear to have been hundreds of such small fortifications during the Middle Ages.

Granary of the Schulte Brüning farm with its exterior stairs at the front, the backside shows a lavatory attachment.

In terms of its construction, this example from Everswinkel is one of the most striking to be found anywhere in North Germany. The upper storey and the roof are jettied on all four sides, and to an exceptional degree. The triple curved elaborately carved and unusually robust wooden brackets which support the gable jetty are particularly beautiful. Perhaps the most interesting features of this building, however, are the thin wooden slats at the foot of each wall post in the upper gable wall. Whilst their primary purpose was to protect the exposed ends of the ceiling joists, they are also forms of architectural decoration. There is only one other known example of this type of construction in Westphalia, and that is in Greven near Münster.

The first floor can only be reached by means of an external staircase. The ornate leaded lights and the lavatory annex in the rear gable indentify this part of the building as potential living space.

K 7 Bleaching hut

from the Deipenbrock farm
in Everswinkel-Schuter in the district of Warendorf,
built around 1860,
dismantled in 1971 and re-erected in 1972

The bleaching equipment was kept in a small hut at the far end of the bleaching field. The hut also served as a shelter for the person watching over the linen at night. The lengths of linen were laid out on the field during the day and had to be kept constantly moist whilst bleaching in the sun. They were left out at night to soak up the dew. For the past 50 years the bleaching hut has been used as shelter-shed for cattle.

*The bleaching hut
in the garden
of the moated farm*

113

K 8 Apiary

(planned)

K 9 Through-passage barn

from the Füstmann farm
in Senden-Schölling in the district of Coesfeld,
built in 1796,
dismantled in 1964 and re-erected in 1969 – 70

Barns, granaries and sheds resting on pyramid-shaped stone staddles capped with coping stones are a fairly common sight in many parts of Europe, including Portugal, Switzerland, England and Scandinavian. Most oft those to be found in Westphalia are concentrated in the Münsterland area (see: Farm from West Münsterland). These so-called "Musepiler" (mouse pillars) staddle-stones were designed primarily to protect the contents of the building from vermin, but they also facilitated good ventilation.

This large through-passage barn in which oats were stored stands on its own small island and is surrounded by a moat which is partially grassed over. The two central bays are open, forming transverse passages from which the two outer bays were loaded with oats. The walls of this timber-framed structure are strengthened by angle braces and are not infilled with brick or wattle and daub, but are covered with plain weatherboarding. The only trace of ornamentation is provided by the curved and slightly recessed boards at the apex of the gable, capped with a pretty flower, and by the inscription above the larger of the two entrances.

JOHAN . HENRICH . DUTSCH . GENANT ESSELMANN .
UND . ANNA . MARIA . SOLCK EHELEUTE DIE .
HABEN . DIESES . HAUS . ERNEUERT: DEN . 12. JULIY
ANNO 1796

The through-passage
barn on its mouse pillar
staddle-stones

K 10 Pigsty

from Martinistraße 11,
Greven in the district of Steinfurt,
built in the 17th century,
dismantled in 1960 and re-erected in 1969 – 70

Because of their exceptionally strong and unpleasant smell, pigs were not
kept in the farmhouse but were provided whenever possible with their own
quite separate accommodation.

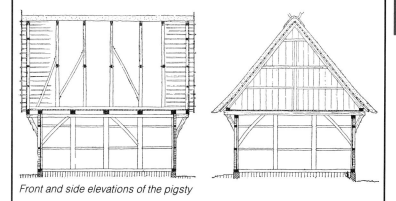

Front and side elevations of the pigsty

A small outbuilding from Greven serves as the pigsty on this
moated farm in the museum. It stands on a base of high sandstone plinth, which prevents the acrid dung from rotting the
ground sills. The broad roof, which is jettied on all four sides
and rests on an array of elaborately carved brackets, is typical
of the kind found on the older generation of timber-framed
buildings. It protects the walls and sills from the rain.

K 11 Lavatory

based on an example from the 19th century,
built in 1978.
Heart stone taken from a 19th century lavatory.

K 12 Sheepfold

from the Berlage farm
in Wettringen-Dorfbauerschaft
in the district of Steinfurt,
rebuilt around 1971 and re-erected in 1981

Sheep were kept on many farms for their wool, meat and manure, provided there was enough common pasture land, or owned fallow field such as heathland and moors or hedgerows on which they could graze.

With a front gable wall measuring 10.7 metres across and eaves walls that are 9.75 metres in length, this sheepfold is broader than it is long. Between November and April it provided shelter for a herd of more than 100 sheep, and from March onwards 80 lambs as well. To protect the timberwork from the caustic effects of the dung, the building was raised on a platform on sandstone plinths. The dung was allowed to remain in situ throughout the winter where it combined with the straw bedding to form an ever increasing mound of manure. This explains why the doors of sheepfolds always open outwards. One of the doors displays a particularly old-fashioned feature: It has wooden hinges which in turn pivot in wooden sockets. As can be seen from the ends of the beams which are joined to the tops of the posts in the eaves wall, as much of the tree as possible was used in the construction of this building. They are in fact the root bales of an oak tree. The large-framing of the walls is further evidence of the fact that timber was a scare and expensive commodity.

K 13 Day-labourer's cottage

(planned)

L 1 Krummes Haus (Crooked House)

Büchenberg, Detmold,
in the district of Lippe,
built around 1680

The "Krummes Haus", so-called because of its curved structure, was built in 1680 as an orangery. In 1671 the Countess Amalie zur Lippe acquired the Pöppinghausen estate, which is now the site of the Open Air Museum, with a view to taking up residence there, cultivating its land and creating a small park. It was in the grounds of this park, at the edge of its uppermost terrrace, that the "Krummes Haus" was built. In the course of the 18th century the park, which became known as Friedrichstal, developed into a vast complex of outbuildings, terraces and ponds, most of which has disappeared since the 19th century. As part of the extensive alterations which took place in 1924, the "Krummes Haus" was given a mansard roof and a new timber-framed extension. It is intended to reconstruct the house and to restore the terraced grounds to their former Baroque glory.

The "crooked house" painted by Albert Michels. The painting is shown in the
"Lippisches Landesmuseum"   *1913*

L 2 Pheasantry

historical animal park in Detmold
in the district of Lippe,
built between 1836 – 38

Pheasants are known to have been reared on the site of the Friedrichstal park as long ago as the early 18th century, and in 1836 the princes zur Lippe decided to re-establish the practice. By 1838 a building had been constructed for this purpose. It was divided into three sections: The slightly projecting middle section was the pheasant keeper's living quarters, whilst those either side of it housed the pheasants themselves. It was built at a cost of 1,800 Reichstaler, and according to the tender the following materials were used in its construction: quarry-stone for the foundations and outer walls; dressed sandstone for the door and window jambs; slate and tiles for the roof; timber framing for the interior walls and clay bricks for infilling; and lime, sand, clay and straw for lining the walls and the ceiling.
The pheasantry, which it is hoped to re-stock, and the "crooked house" are the only two surviving buildings from the former royal estate in the Museum.

Pheasantry of the prince zur Lippe prior to its restoration

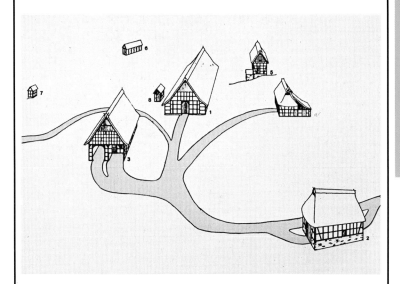

The area which incorporates the former bishopric of Osnabrück has been part of Westphalia since the Middle Ages. In the wake of the political upheavals of the early 19th century, this episcopal estate was annexed to what was later to become the kingdom of Hannover, which today accounts for a considerable part of the federal "Land" of Niedersachsen (Lower Saxony).

The bishopric of Osnabrück extended from the highland borders of the Teutoburger Wald and the Wiehengebirge to the North German plain. The complex of buildings in the Open Air Museum is typical of the kind of farmstead which might have been found on the northern slopes of the Wiehengebirge. The main buildings are situated on an incline at the edge of the wood so that the heavily laden harvest wagons could take full advantage of the gentle gradient leading down to the farmhouse and the barn. The smaller outbuildings are located on slightly higher ground but still allocated to the farm yard.

The walls of the timber-framed buildings in this region are infilled with wattle and daub and finished with a coat of lime-wash. Whereas the older buildings are thatched, the later ones have pantile roofs (a pattern adopted from the Münsterland). In the course of the 18th century these buildings developed a distinctive and easily recognisable style of their own: the gable walls are characterised by close-framed panelling, with that in the pediment often being diamond-shaped. The horizontal timbers are frequently endowed with elaborately carved inscription plates. Yet another typical feature of 18th century farmsteads is the garden with its pyramid-shaped yew bushes and its borders lined with box trees. The summerhouse was also an integral part of such gardens. A huge drystone wall supports the terraced garden.

O 1 Farmhouse

from the Grosse-Endebrock farm
in Bramsche-Kalkriese in the district of Osnabrück,
built in 1609,
dismantled in 1962 and re-erected in 1967 – 68

This farmstead, with its exceptionally large aisled hall-house (35 × 15 metres), once presided over more than 100 hectares of land. Until well into the 19th century the occupants of self-sufficient farms such as this one – the so-called "Vollbauer" (holding a large farm) – had full use of large parts of common land, which included fields, woods and water. Those with smaller farms had a proportionately smaller share, and the peasants and "day-labourers" generally had no rights to common land at all ("Allmende"/"Mark").

The steeply-pitched front gable of this building, which is half timberframed and half weatherboarded, represents an interesting transitional form somewhere between the plunging thatched roof of the 16th century and the steep half-timbered gable which was a familiar sight in towns during the 17th century. The inscription above the main door is dedicated to the original owners:

ANNO 1609 had herman Endebroch: ANNA sin hausfraw die habt dies haus bouwen lathen.

Rear view of the Osnabrück farm showing the bakehouse, pigsty, farmhouse and barn

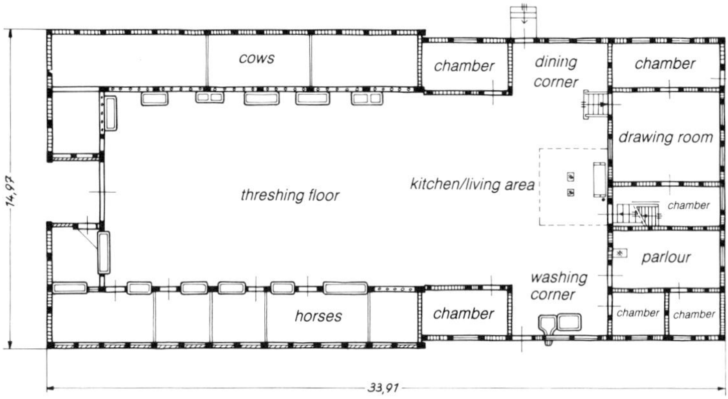
cows
chamber
dining corner
chamber
drawing room
threshing floor
kitchen/living area
chamber
parlour
washing corner
horses
chamber
chamber
chamber
14,97
33,91

If one stands at the large entrance to the threshing floor one gains a marvellous overview of the layout of a typical North German hall-house: A spacious hall extends through to the hearth wall, comprising at its front end a clay threshing floor flanked on either side by animal stalls and at the rear end the main living area, which spans the full distance between the outer walls. The exceptional width of the threshing floor, which measures 9 metres across between the slightly inwardly inclined wall posts at the working end of the building both contribute to the sense of space:

Dismantling of the farm house Grosse-Endebrock *1962*

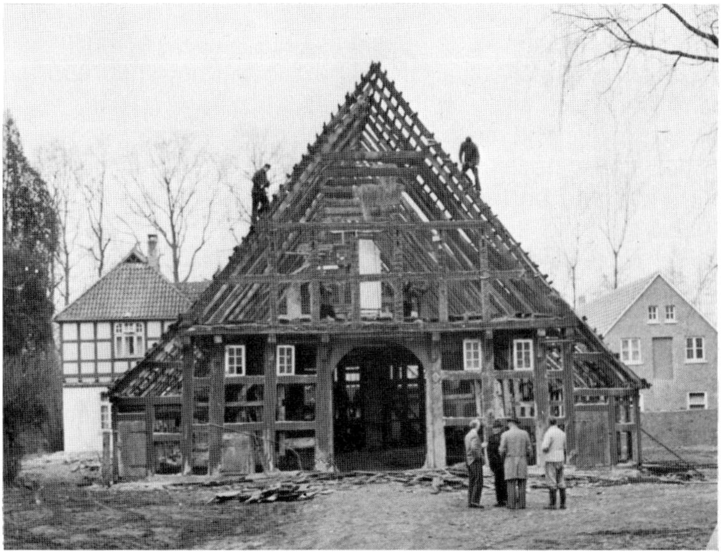

Open dining area in the farm house

The threshing floor, with cattle stalls to its left and stables to its right, comprised the working part of the house. It was used every day for chopping animal fodder, and the dung from the stalls was deposited here before being taken away in a wheelbarrow. From here the harvested crops could be transferred directly from the cart to the loft above. The threshing floor was even used for weddings, funerals and other occasional festivities. The servants' sleeping quarters are situated at the far end of the animal stalls, the maids' next to the cowshed and the farm labourers' adjoining the stables.

At the lower end of the hall is the kitchen-cum-living area, which spans the full width of the building. On the left is the dining table and on the opposite wall, the washing area, which looks out onto the well. Next to the table, to the left of the bench-seat, stands a built-in bread cupboard which carries the following inscription: **ALLER AUGEN WARTEN AUF DICH HER DEN 12. JULI 1799.** To the left of the small flight of steps is a sideboard with open shelves. A plate-rack carrying wooden plates and soup ladles is attached to the wall post opposite. Next to the butter churn in the washing corner is a wash-tub, and directly above the sink is a draining rack for the crockery. Alongside it stands a stone water container, and the shaving mirror on the post above confirms that this area was also used for maintaining personal hygiene.

Linen cupboards were standard pieces of household furniture, and they were fitted with wheels to enable them to be removed from the house in the event of a fire. Indeed, they were known colloquially as "fire cupboards". The chest opposite, which is equipped with handles, would appear to be easier to move, but when full it requires the combined strength of several people to lift it.

The "kitchen" was both the main work-room for the women of the house and the principal living room for all the family. This is perhaps not surprising given that the open fire was not only the sole means of cooking, but also the only source of heat and light. The smoke from the fire was not extracted by a chimney but wafted freely about the house. There is a flat deflector above the hearth to prevent flying sparks, and the smoke which billowed from either side of it cured the sausages and other meats which hung from the ceiling: it also helped keep the cereals in the loft dry. The various implements in and around the hearth were mainly cooking utensils. The burning logs rested on a pair of iron fire-dogs, whilst those pots and pans which could not be placed directly on the fire were suspended above it on a height adjustable hook or "crane" attached to a large hinge. Since there was only one fireplace, only one pot could be heated at a time, and the staple dish therefore tended to be a kind of stew or "hot-pot". The fire was also used for heating the animal feed.

Other small utensils are hanging from the hearth wall. The stone bench next to the fire provided both a warm place to sit and somewhere to deposit the wood ash, which was used for making lye.

Until the beginning of the 18th century the house terminated at the present hearth wall. It was subsequently extended to incorporate a suite of chambers, and also acquired a new rear gable which displays the decorative closely framed half-timbering so characteristic of this period. A shallow cellar was added around the same time.

Said cellar is the reason why the "drawing room", which also served as the master bedroom, is only accessible by means of a staircase. This room was not heated, and the various devices which people used to keep warm — a small metal container filled with embers, a "warming stone", a warming pan and a hot-water bottle — are displayed here. The furniture in the drawing room is typical of the style which emerged in rural areas during the 18th century.

The window overlooking the kitchen and the threshing floor allowed the farmer or his wife to keep a watchful eye on the servants and animals at night or when one of them was ill. An emergency door in the adjoining room on the left provided a means of escape in the event of a fire.

The only heated room in the house was the parlour, which is remarkably small for a farm of this size. This would tend to suggest that, unlike the drawing room and the "kitchen", the parlour was not used a great deal in the region around Osnabrück until well into the 19th century. The remaining chambers served as sleeping quarters for the retired members of the family and the staff. The door next to the fireplace gives on to a set of wooden steps which lead up to the storage space in the loft.

O 2 Sheepfold

from the Grosse-Endebrock farm
in Bramsche-Kalkriese
in the district of Osnabrück,
built in 1792,
dismantled in 1966 and re-erected in 1967

The sheepfold from Kalkriese before being dismantled   *1966*

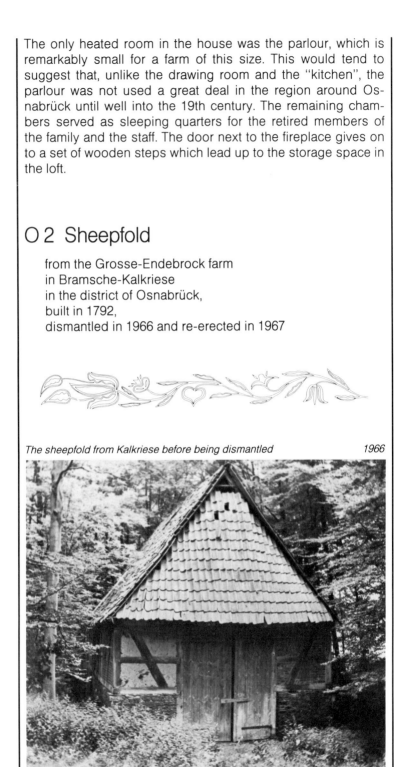

The sheepfold is situated in a wood some distance away from the other buildings on the Osnabrück farm, just as it was at its previous site. It comprises one large room which could easily accommodate up to a hundred sheep, and was used mainly in the winter. The high quarry stone plinth wall on which it stands prevented the urine from rotting the timber frame, and without it the building would not have lasted very long at all. The ventilation slits in the walls help disperse the vapour given off by the sheep. The gable facing in the direction of the farm bears the following decorative inscription:

Anna Maria Adelheit Stiewers, Witwe, Grose Endebroks, Johan Herbort Grose Endebrock, Anno, 1792, den, 8. Juni

The inscription on the rear gable reads:

Mst. J. H. Borggelt,   Wie soll ich den Herrn Vergelten alle seine Wohltaht die er an mir Thut Psalm ...

Both gables are shielded from the rain by a semi-conical roof. The sheepfold has become a working building again in the museum, although the herd is now only 25 strong.

O 3 Barn

from the Osthaar farm
in Bissendorf-Holte-Sünsbeck
in the district of Osnabrück,
built in 1763,
dismantled and re-erected in 1967

For a working building this barn is very decoratively constructed. The gables above the two open gable entrances consist of several small jetties and are criss-crossed with close-framed panels of the type commonly found in the Osnabrück region in the 18th century.
At ground level the barn housed a variety of farm vehicles (wagons, carts and sledges) and a number of large agricultural implements (e.g. a cattle cart, a land roller and a harrow). The loft space was used for storing cereals.
The partition wall clearly shows the different stages involved in the infilling of a timber-framed wall with wattle and daub.

Barn and farmhouse viewed from the farmyard gate

The long swinging beam lined with iron prongs which is attached to this wall was used for stripping the seed capsules from the flax stalks. The bressumer on the gable facing the farm carries the following Biblical inscription:

Habe deine Lust an dem Herrn der Wirdt Dir geben Was dein Hertze Wünschelt Befiell dem Herrn deine Wege und Hoffe auf ihn Err Wirdt es Woll Machen Psallm 37 V 4.5

The inscription on the arch above the door reads:

Johan Hinrich Tieman genandt Kuhlenbecke und Catrina Maria Kuhlenbecke
Anno 1763 den 27   Novenber Meist. J. H. W. in

O 4 Pigsty

from the Strietmann farm,
in Bramsche-Schleptrup
in the district of Osnabrück,
built in 1827,
dismantled in 1966 and re-erected in 1967

Pigsty from Schleptrup

Pigs were normally kept in purpose-built sties. They were not welcome in the house because of their smell and the noise they made. This particular building is an open-fronted, multi-purpose shed in which fuel supplies (turf and wood) were stored until well into the 19th century. The actual pigsty, with its quarry stone walls, is attached to the rear of the shed. The building also sheltered several pieces of garden and farm equipment (a plough, a drill hoe and a wheelbarrow). It differs from the other buildings on the farm inasmuch as the main entrance is located in the eaves wall and not in the gable. There is a decorative inscription on the lintel above the door:

Johan Hinrich Funke, Maria Adelheit Haubenings

An 1827   Mstr Ch

d 22 Juni   Nieman

The bulging roof provides an ideal shelter for farm vehicles. The carved inscription on the left-hand gable gives an insight into the trials and tribulations of an 18th century farmer:

Herr, ich bin das Bauen müde, Erhalt in Ruh und Frieden
von Brand und allen schaden, Herr, unsern Bau in Gnaden

127

O 5 Bakehouse granary

from the Koke farm
in Ostercappeln-Schwagstorf
in the district of Osnabrück,
built in 1710,
dismantled in 1966 and re-erected in 1967 – 68

The slope on which this bakehouse granary (bakehouse with storage room) stands is so steep that it was possible to convert the stone base of the building into an easily accessible ground-level cellar, which was used for storing oil, coal and, from the end of the 18th century, potatoes too.

The two clay baking vaults, which are not fitted with chimneys, are attached to the outside of the bakehouse; the larger one was heated at intervals of several weeks for baking bread, and was also used for drying fruit or (illegally) flax after it had been soaked or "retted" in the dyke. The smaller vault could be used for baking "white" bread or cakes without consuming too much wood. The smoke that resulted when the oven was being heated escaped through the wooden grill above the door.

In addition to the standard baking equipment (kneading trough, fire rake bread ladle etc.), the baking room also contains presses for extracting honey from the comb. The inscription on the lintel above the door is totally illegible in places:

Bakehouse with
storage room

Hans Hinricht Alwig genant Pocke
und..................... Pocken anno 1810

The one on the door post reads:

... CKSCHE
DEN 3 MAI
Anno 1710

It is possible that the more recent of the two dates denotes the year in which alterations were made to the building.
There is a further inscription on the tiebeam of the gable pediment:

WER GOT VERTRAVWET DER HAT WOL GEBAVWET
IM HIMEL VND AVF ERDEN WER SICH VERLEST
AVF JESVH CHRIST DEM WIRD DER HIMEL
WERDEN AMEN M. JOHAN ...

O 6 Apiary

from the Reckfort farm
in Warmsen-Hauskämpen
in the district of Nienburg,
built around 1860,
dismantled and re-erected in 1968

Apiary in the garden of the farm house

At the bottom of the garden is a large apiary, which is open on one side and houses about 25 beehives. It is a comparatively recent example and is typical of many others to be found scattered across north-east Westphalia. Like those of the two other 19th century buildings on the farm, the timber-framed walls are infilled not with wattle and daub, but with brick, and the roof is similarly covered with pantiles.

In Germany beet sugar has only been produced in any quantity since 1830, and the only sweeteners available before then were expensive American cane sugar or domestically produced honey.

Bleaching hut prior to being dismantled in Gersten in 1967

O 7 Bleaching Hut

from the Scheepers-Beestermöller farm
in Gersten in the district of Lingen,
built around 1840,
dismantled and re-erected in 1967

Down the slope, to the left of the garden, lies the bleaching field. The small, modestly constructed building at its edge, whose timber frame comprises several naturally curved pieces of wood, is the bleaching hut. It contained the equipment used in the bleaching process, such as scoops for watering the linen as it basked in the sun, and also served as a shelter for the person guarding the linen at night.

O 8 Lavatory

based on a 19th century design and built in 1968

Lavatories housed in separate buildings are a comparatively recent development. Until the 19th century, the rural population was obliged to use the animal stalls, where in-built lavatories can occasionally still be found.

O 9 Potter's workshop

from the Rhotert farm, Hehemann pottery,
Hagen-Gellenbeck, district of Osnabrück,
built in 1828;
dismantled in 1976, re-erected in 1982 – 84

The region of Osnabrück is one of the traditional pottery areas of Germany. There is evidence of small medieval workshops around Iburg/Dissen and in the Habicht forest near Tecklenburg having produced pottery for the local demand. In Natrup-Hagen, a hamlet within the Hagen parish, pottery was made in the 16th and 17th centuries.

In the 18th century — the age of mercantilism — the Osnabrück pottery trade was promoted by the state, but it reached its most productive state as late as in the middle of the 19th century when the "Ossenbrügger gschir" (pottery from Osnabrück) had a widespread renown, not limited to the Osnabrück region.

Potter Hehemann's workshop prior to being dismantled   *1974*

Pottery workshop with its drying and wood sheds

Ever since the end of the 18th century at the latest, the municipality of Hagen/ T. W. was the pottery centre of the Osnabrück region comprising almost 20 families involved with pottery, as ascertained for the period from 1768 to 1949.

Trade statistics of 1818 reveal first feasible figures about the production capacity of the eight workshops in Hagen. One of the large workshops baked 10 times in 1818, the other seven baked 5 times each. According to the 1818 statistics, the eight workshops in Hagen yielded an annual production of 9200 lots or 46 000 pieces, after deduction of 15% rejects. Fifteen years later, the number of workshops in Hagen had risen from eight to eleven, including the Hehemann pottery.

The prosperous years around 1850 were followed by several decades of decline, due to a rapidly expanding supply of mass products of earthenware, chinaware, moulded glass, sheet metal or cast iron. Around 1900, Hagen counted merely three pottery workshops, seven were left in the Osnabrück area (now rural district and town of Osnabrück). Until 1949, the Hehemann pottery was in operation, being the second last workshop of the Osnabrück area, and one of the last to represent the trade in Northern Germany.

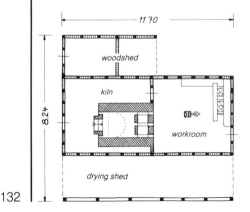

The man who founded the Hehemann workshop on the premises of the semi entailed Rhotert farm in the Goldbach valley was Johann Hermann Henrich Hehemann, born in 1784 who died in 1855 in Gellenbeck. He was a hired labourer or tenant for pay of the farm of Meyer zu Spelbrink and built the workshop in 1828. The inscription on the gable pediment reads:

HERMANN HENRICH HEHEMANN UND
CATHARINA MARIA WORPENBERG EHELEUTE
DEN 12 NOV 1828.

The weather worn inscription on the lintel may give the name of the carpenter:

M W (?) SCHMID

Hehemann's pottery workshop is a half timbered house, 11.70 meters in length and 5.30 m wide. The wall structure with is double nogging and the curved bottom braces at the corner posts rests on a quarry stone plinth. The plain rafter roof is covered with pantiles and shows low extensions at both sides. The outer walls were partly painted in a light blue until the thirties of the 20th century, and so they are now in the open air museum. Inside, the house is divided into two rooms, the square shaped workshop and the kiln room. The kiln now re-erected in the workshop has been reconstructed after the measurements of the last kiln. The older kiln which was operated until 1929 had a volume of 5.7 cubic meters and its capacity was higher than that of the later one erected in its place measuring merely 4.2 cubic meters.

Pottery was not a trade to live on. The potter had to have a second trade to secure his livelihood. Like many other country craftsmen, he had to cover his subsistence from the products and proceeds of his own farm. As his ancestors, the last potter, master Wilhelm Hehemann, was a hired labourer and remained such until he died in 1960. The farmhouse, workshop, vegetable garden and orchard, fields and clay pits were let to him by farmer Rhotert. The rent was kept small. In return, Hehemann had to give the farmer „dubbelte hölpe up unbestemde tid" (double help for an undetermined period of time), i.e. to make the manpower of two adult persons available wherever help was required.

The selling range of the Hehemann workshop was never more than 30 km. On October 1, 1949 Wilhelm Hehemann had his workshop taken off the role at the Chamber of Crafts in Osnabrück.

P 1 – 2 Kotten (Farm-labourers' cottages)

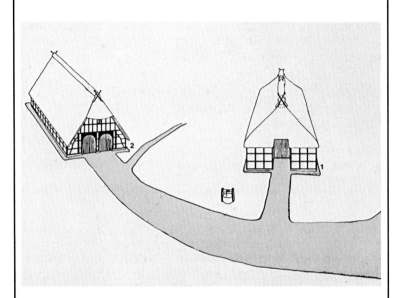

In the main, "cottages" were small dwellings inhabited by those members of the rural community who were not farmers. Those in the Open Air Museum were the homes of "day-labourers", who constituted the lowest social class in rural Westphalia living in a separate house. A day-labourer who wanted to get married and secure a home of his own as a rule had to be ‚hired' by a farmer, and this would possibly have enabled him to progress a little further up the social ladder.

These small houses were built by the owners of large and middle-sized farms as a ready source of labour for themselves. They were supplied with a house, a small garden and some arable land on a fixed lease in return for rent and labour.

Since his small plot of land did not provide him with an adequate livelihood, the peasant was obliged either to work on the owner's farm or to find some other job. In either case, his wife and children had to lend a hand, too.

In areas where there were a lot of day-labourers (and their numbers increased towards the end of the 17th century, particularly in the regions of Osnabrück, Minden-Ravensberg and Lippe), there was not always enough work to go round, with the result that many of them became itinerant workers (most of them went to Holland) or craftsmen (e. g. carpenters or cobblers).

The most common form of domestic work in these areas was linen-making (spinning and/or weaving). Due to competition from cheaper English cotton textiles in the early part of the 19th century, the production of linen went into a steady decline, and this had a dramatic effect on the lives of the day-labourers and their families. Since the buyers were constantly forcing down the price and there was no other avaible work, they were reduced to miserable living and working conditions. Only in the late 19th century, as a result of emigration and the gradual exodus of people from the land to the towns and cities were the day-labourers able to improve their economic position. There continued to be day-labourers in Germany after the Second World War.

P 1 The Tecklenburg cottage

from the Niesing farm
in Mettingen-Höveringhausen
in the district of Steinfurt,
built in 1784,
dismantled in 1967 and re-erected in 1967 – 68

The main source of income on this small-holding was not agriculture but domestic handicrafts. Here flax was turned into fibre, from which thread was spun and woven into linen. The men-folk would hawk the finished product across the countryside, often on their backs. This form of itinerant trade flourished in the 18th century but gradually declined in the 19th century.

The exterior of the house displays certain characteristics which point to the low social status of its inhabitants. For example, in the late 18th century such a low roof was only to be found on small "cottages". Farmhouses, on the other hand, had been endowed with steeply pitched gables for some considerable time. On this particular house the roof extends down as far as the low doorway. Equally typical are the plaited straw crosses at the tips of the gables. And nowhere else would a pigsty be found inside the house (on the right, next to the door). The walls are infilled with sandstone from the nearby Teutoburger Wald.

The fireplace and chimney were installed sometimes after 1830, following a trend which had begun in the Münsterland.

The Tecklenburg cottage in Höveringhausen   *1967*

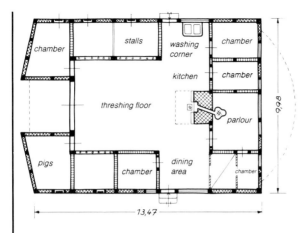

The arrangement of the various rooms is indicative of the over-whelming importance of textiles in this house: there is a weaving room to the left of the main entrance and another on the left at the rear of the building. The loft space up on the right contains large piles of flax stalks.

Unlike the agricultural day-labourer, who often received payment in kind, the itinerant linen trader (his back-pack is on top of the cupboard on the right) earned cash from the goods he sold with which he could then afford to buy things that were beyond the means of the day-labourer — assuming, of course,

Heating and cooking store in the parlour of the Tecklenburg cottage

Wall bed to be closed by sliding doors, a sleeping place which was considered old fashioned as early as in the 18th century.

that business was brisk. One such purchase was the iron stove in the parlour, which was used both for heating and cooking, and another is the Black Forest clock which was in turn acquired from itinerant traders.

The living area is extremely small, particularly when one considers that it probably had to accommodate three generations of a family. The living conditions at that time must have been cramped, to say the least.

The inscription on the beam directly above the stove confirms that the man who owned this cottage provided his sister and her husband with some of the materials used in its construction:

Anno 1784 13 July Johan Hinrich Hiller Man Gib Diesen Balken zum Haus

The names of the people who first occupied the cottage and the the date when it was built can be seen on the lintel above the door:

Johan Petter Meier genant Hiller + Man
und Anna Catrina Hiller Mans + /
Das Heil der Welt + Herr Jesus Christ in Hostia warhafftig
ist im sacra/ment das hochste Gut + verborgen liegt im
fleisch und Blut
Anno 1784   13 July

The Tecklenburg cottage on its original site   1967

The Tecklenburg cottage after reconstruction

P 2 Doppelheuerhaus (Two family cottage)

from the Reiner farm
in Bad Essen-Hüsede in the district of Osnabrück,
built in 1609/1738,
dismantled in 1967 and re-erected in 1968

This building resulted from the reconstruction of a small and much older farmhouse in 1738. Its basic structure, except for the door in the left-hand side-wall and the partition wall, which was inserted shortly after it was built, is that of a 16th century aisled house. The old portal was subsequently moved further to the right, and the side walls and rear gable were replaced in the 18th century. This was the only cottage on the Reiner farm — which was located on the outskirts of the village of Hüsede — and it is situated about 1,000 metres from the main house. The partition wall which divides the building into two equal halves meant that it could be let to two "hired" families. Indeed, it continued to be occupied by two parties until as late as 1932. It was not unknown for the farmer and his wife to move into one half of the house when they retired. The day-labourers were tied to the Reiner farm, and their wives and children were likewise obliged to work for the owner. Even in the 20th century the day-labourer was required to do between 50 and 70 days' work a year on his master's estate.
It is known that two such peasant families occupied this cottage around 1770; one of them had five children, whilst the other comprised a married couple, a child and a grandmother.

The threshing floor in the "Doppelheuerhaus". In the background is the kitchen with its fireplace and the door leading into the parlour.

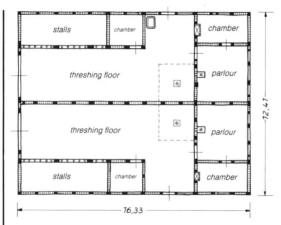

At the beginning of the 19th century the rent for each half of the house was 4 taler a year, whilst that for the accompanying three acres of land was 10 taler. We also know how many animals there were around 1900: Each family owned a cow, a she-goat, a couple of pigs and few hens. During the economic depression of the mid-19th century, one of the families joined the many others who were emigrating to America.

The layout of the two halves of the house is similar to that found in other hall-houses: Beyond the main door are the animal stalls and the threshing floor where most of the domestic and farm work was done. The meagre fireplace in the small "kitchen" does not have a chimney. But as in most other houses, the narrow parlour is heated from the threshing floor by an iron stove. There are two bedrooms, one for the parents,

The front gable of the "Doppelheuerhaus" with its two main entrances

the other for the grandparents. The children were forced to sleep up on the "stage" above the parlour. The arch over the main door on the right carries the house number, N 2.

The following inscription appears above the left-hand door:

Pilip Tefes   und Anna Sophia Busch
ANNO 1738   den 22 May
ANNO   1764
Den 28   May

The rear gable of the "Doppelheuerhaus" at its original site in Hüsede   *1967*

The "Doppelheuerhaus" being dismantled   *1967*

Q 1 – 8 Farmstead from Minden

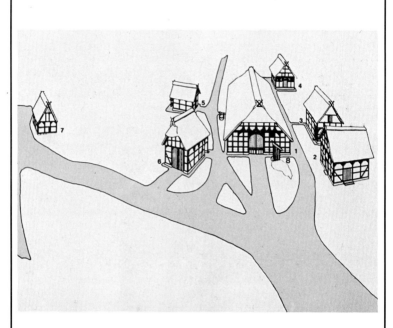

Most of the buildings on this farmstead originally came from the former prince-bishopric of Minden. The latter was annexed to Brandenburg in 1648, which in turn later became part of Prussia. The greater part of this territory lies on a plain to the north of the Wiehengebirge, which once formed the north-east tip of Westphalia in the Weserbergland. It consisted mostly of heath and moor-land. In the museum, the group of buildings dating from the 17th century relate to a middle-sized pastoral farm of approximately 100 acres of land.

Typical of the buildings in this region are the foundations composed of irregular block-stones, the extremely ornate timber-framing (e. g. the curved angle braces in the gable wall of the farmhouse) and the hipped roofs, all of which were thatched and had ridges consisting of a thick covering of heather. The walls are infilled with wattle and daub. At the front the farmyard is bordered with a raised bed of plants and over by the garden with a wicker-work fence.

Q 1 Farmhouse

from the Bussing/Brandt farm
in Raddestorf-Kleinenheerse
in the district of Nienburg,
built in 1673,
dismantled in 1966 and re-erected in 1968 – 69

The front gable of this middle-sized farmhouse with its half-hipped roof and ornamental horses heads at its apex is typically that of a North German hall-house. The slightly recessed portal and the side walls of the stables together form a kind of porch where the horses could be harnessed and unharnessed in the dry. When the main door was open the house could still be closed off to freely-roaming domestic animals by a decorative lattice work door.

The inscriptions on the gable timbers provide details about the original owners of the farm:

GOTT IST VNSER BESCHVTZER
(DER HERR BEHVTE DEINEN) EINGANG VON NVN
AN BIS IN EWIGKEIT   ANNO 1673   GOTT GESEGNE
DIS HAVS VND ALLE (DIE DA GEHEN EIN VND AVS)
TILEKE · BUSSINGK   ILSCHE · BUSCHKINGK

The arrangement of the stables allowed more space to be given over to cows and bullocks, reflecting the importance of 55pastoral farming in the damp climate of the Weser basin to the north of Minden. The stalls on either side of the clay threshing floor provided accommodation for about 20 bullocks. Next to the loose-boxes (designed to take up to 5 horses) is everything necessary for the welfare of these animals: a large oat bin, harnesses and wooden shoes designed specifically to cope with soft ground. On the left-hand side of the threshing floor is a threshing machine.

The Bussing/Brandt Farm in Kleinenherse   *before 1935*

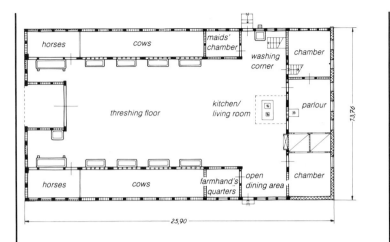

The pegs which line the drum act like small flails, beating the corn out of the ears. Machines of this kind became commonplace during the late 19th century and made the job of threshing considerably easier. They were driven by an ingenious system of gears, the power being provided by a horse. Before the inventions of such machines, a certain quantity of corn had to be threshed by hand every morning before breakfast during the winter months. The corn was then stored in the granary, whilst the seed was put into large woven baskets which were kept in the loft, an open space on top of the stalls. Here we get an insight into some of the less pleasant aspects of life in a North German hall-house which has occasionally been over-romanticised.

View of the threshing floor from the fireplace

In addition to the familiar smells and noises produced by the
animals, there were other nuisances to be endured, such as
the dust given off during the threshing process — and all within a stone's throw of the kitchen and dining area! There are two
cabinets on the threshing floor — the one on the left is a
crockery cupboard with carved lattice-work doors, whilst that
on the right is a highly ornate linen-cupboard. They were both
too tall to be kept in any of the living rooms.

A beautiful floor composed of countless pebbles distinguishes
the living area from the working end of the building. In front of
the fireplace the year in which it was laid — 1828 — has been
immortalised across four pebbled panels.

A folding bench is attached to the end wall post on the right-
hand side. It was used by day-labourers and voluntary helpers
at harvest time or during the threshing season when there
were not enough chairs to go round. The layout of the main
living area is similar to that found in other hallhouses. The
open washing area on the left lies directly opposite the dining
area, where chests serve as traditional rural seats. Over on the
left by the window is a cleverly designed drop-leaf table which
also converted into a seat, the raised leaf serving as a back
rest.

Heated parlours had been a feature of houses in the Minden
area since the 16th century, and here too the stove (made in
1745) was supplied with heat from the kitchen/living area.

The farmer and his family slept in beds which were let into the
wall and framed with rich and colourful surrounds (a feature of
the 18th and 19th centuries). When drawn, the curtains which
were draped across the foot of each bed helped keep in the
body heat given off by the occupants, and were not therefore
solely for decoration. These box-beds had doors which opened on to the adjacent spinning room. When both curtains and
doors were open, the heat from the parlour was thus able to

The box-beds in the parlour on the Minden farm

percolate through to the spinning room. This arrangement also enabled the farmer to keep a close eye on the antics of his staff from the comfort of his bed.

The elderly members of the family lived under the same roof as the farmer and occupied the chamber to the left of the parlour. The door on the left next to the entrance to the parlour conceals the staircase leading up to the corn loft, which can be seen from the grandparents' bedroom. Among other things, the spinning room contains a chest which comes from the Vierlanden near Hamburg. It is inlaid with both light and dark wood, and its rather peculiar appearance sets it apart from the rest of the furniture. In 18th century Minden the larger pieces of furniture tended to be richly carved and brightly coloured, and even the smaller items such as chairs were highly elaborate and colourful. The chest to which we have referred was a much sought-after import in this region during the 19th century (arriving via the rivers Elbe and Weser).

During the course of structural alterations which took place towards the end of the 18th century, the house acquired a cellar and a solid rear wall, which was built in two stages and bears the precise year when the modifications were carried out:

Johann Gerhard Bußing Margareta Sophie Ruraden. ANNO 1780. M. Conrad Heinrich Bussing. Dennoch bleibe ich stets an dir, denn du haltest mich bey meiner rechten Hand. Du leitest mich nach deinem Rath.

Q 2 Granary

from the Bödeker farm
in Rahden in the district of Minden-Lübbecke,
built in 1712,
dismantled in 1967 and re-erected in 1968 – 69

As granaries go, this single-storey building is exceptionally small. But since this was a predominantly pastoral farm there was no need for a large grain store. The curved corner braces give the outer walls a slightly rounded appearance. The jettied gable pediment, which is protected by weatherboarding, is crowned with a finial. Although it certainly had a structural role to play in reinforcing the apex of the gable, it also developed in the course of time into an effective piece of decoration. The names of the original owners of the building are engraved above the door:

TOMAS JOCHIM HOLING
CATRIN ANGENESE   SPRADAM ELÜDT

The date when it was built can be seen above the side door:

AN GOTTES : SEGEN : IST : ALLES :
GELEGEN : ANNO : DOMINI : 1712 :

Q 3 Pigsty

from the Aumann farm
in Petershagen-Buchholz
in the district of Minden-Lübbecke,
built around 1585,
dismantled in 1968 and re-erected in 1969

Although the pigsty is not attached to the house, it is nevertheless situated fairly close to the kitchen door so that the women did not have far to carry the large pot of swill from the hearth to the through. The ogee arch above the door in the eaves wall is late-Gothic in style. The timberwork also differs considerably from that of the other buildings on the farm. It displays the pegged tenons so characteristic of the somewhat old-fashioned "anchor beam" method of construction. Further examples of this type of building can be seen elsewhere in Westphalia, most notably in west Münsterland.

Q 4 Wood store

from the Kolkhorst farm
in Rahden-Wehe in the district of Minden-Lübbecke,
built around 1625,
dismantled in 1967 and re-erected in 1969

The open wall panels, lined only with slender laths of oak, ensure that the firewood stored in this building is kept well ventilated. The heather in the gable wall serves a similar purpose; it protects the building from the driving rain, but at the same time lets in the drying wind.

Q 5 Bakehouse

from the Brammeyer farm
in Espelkamp-Frotheim
in the district of Minden-Lübbecke,
built in 1614,
dismantled in 1968 and re-erected in 1969

The bakehouse is the only building on the farm whose timber frame is infilled with quarry-stone. The diagonal panel braces are naturally curved lengths of wood.

The bakehouse from Frotheim and its attached oven

Aerial view oft the Minden farm. The two cottages are in the top left-hand corner.

The baking oven with its clay dome rests on a base of powerful oak timbers. Because of the high risk of fire, the roof over the oven vault is covered with pantiles. Inside this building — which, incidentally, does not have a chimney — are all the pieces of equipment one would expect: a baking table, a dough trough and an oven peel.

Except for the date, the inscription above the door is completely illegible: **Anno 1614 . . .**

Q 6 Barn

from the Rieke farm
in Warmsen-Bohnhorst
in the district of Nienberg,
built in 1671;
dismantled and re-erected in 1969

This one-room building can be entered either through a low, open arch in the side wall or through a door in the gable wall. At ground level, it houses vehicles such as carts and sledges with plaited straw bodywork, and a number of agricultural implements such as ploughs and harrows. There was also space in the loft for storing crops.

The inscription over the gable door is particularly interesting:

ANNO 1671 IDER NICHT LEHRT LE VND SCHRIEBEN
DER MVS DER HERNACH OSEN VND (ESEL) DRIEFEN

. . . which in plain English means: "Those who do not learn to
read and write must be content to tend oxen and asses."
The date when the barn was constructed is engraved above
the side entrance:

WIR BAVEN HIR SO FEST VND SIND HIR FROMDE
GEST DA WIR SOLTEN EWICH SEIN DAR DENKN
WIR / GAR WENICH EIN
ANNO 1671 HAT RVDLOF RIEKE HAT EINEN NEVEN
KASTEN BAVEN LASSEN DVRCH M. KORD FINKEN:
AN GOTTES SEGEN IST ALLES GELEHGEN ANNO
1671

Q 7 "Fire Barn"

from the Frölking farm
in Diepenau-Nordel in the district of Nienburg,
built around 1700,
dismantled in 1964 and re-erected in 1970

Situated well away from the farmhouse is the so-called "fire
barn", in which a reserve supply of seed was stored in case of
fire. The gable of this building is also lined with heather to ensure good ventilation. Instead of a door, the barn merely has a
hatch in the front gable.

Q 8 Lavatory

based on a 17th century example,
built in 1975

T 1 – 7 Large farm from Lippe
(Lippischer Meierhof)

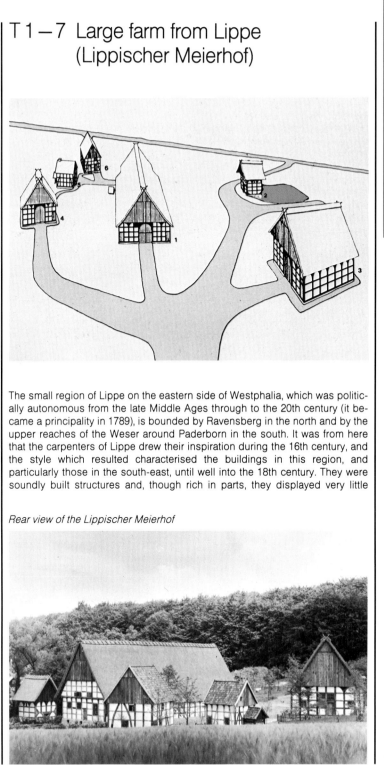

The small region of Lippe on the eastern side of Westphalia, which was politically autonomous from the late Middle Ages through to the 20th century (it became a principality in 1789), is bounded by Ravensberg in the north and by the
upper reaches of the Weser around Paderborn in the south. It was from here
that the carpenters of Lippe drew their inspiration during the 16th century, and
the style which resulted characterised the buildings in this region, and
particularly those in the south-east, until well into the 18th century. They were
soundly built structures and, though rich in parts, they displayed very little

Rear view of the Lippischer Meierhof

151

ornamentation (often restricted to carved brackets in the gable and carved inscriptions over the doors). The lime-washed wattle-and-daub infill and the thatched roofs (which survived until the late 18th century) also contributed to the distinctive appearance of the typical 'lippish' farmstead.

Nestling in the surrounding countryside, this particular farm was built on the site of a pond and is typical of many others to be found scattered across the hill country of northern Lippe, right down to the number and arrangement of the outbuildings around the farmyard.

Until well into the 19th century most country dwellers in the German Reich did not own the land they farmed. It belonged either to the nobility or to the Church and was leased to the peasants in return for taxes and services, which were often very oppressive. One of the legal provisions was the so called "Meier-Law" (Leasehold form common in Northern Germany). Such leasing arrangements had legal status, and although there were of course regional variations, farms were always handed on from father to son. In Lippe, farmers who entered into such a contract were known as "Meier", and they constituted the most important section of the farming community.

T 1 Farmhouse

from the Meier Barthold farm
in Lemgo-Leese in the district of Lippe, built in 1570,
dismantled in 1968 and re-erected between 1971 – 73

This farm, whose house was bequeathed to the Museum by the previous owner, W. Führing, is known to have been in existence as long ago as the 14th century when it belonged to the bishopric of Herford. In the 15th century the estate was divided up into two equal parts, and this house was built on one of them in 1570 (the date can still be seen on the gable wall) from timbers which were possibly intended originally for a barn. Around 1600 a suite of chambers was added above a shallow cellar. During this period the farm had about 65 hectares of land, and according to an inventory compiled in 1604 there were 11 horses, 20 cows and bullocks, 10 pigs and piglets, a flock of sheep and a number of beehives. It was therefore a large and highly productive concern.

The basic elements which go to make up the load-bearing structure are vertical wall posts (a) and horizontal beams (b). Each beam is supported by two posts

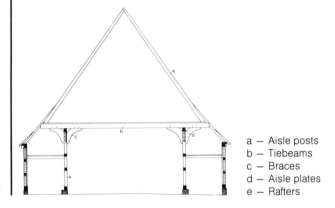

a — Aisle posts
b — Tiebeams
c — Braces
d — Aisle plates
e — Rafters

Farmhouse from Leese on its original site, about 1935

to form a kind of "frame", of which there are ten in all. Continuous lengths of timber known as wall-plates (d) bind the wall posts together. Powerful angle braces (c) at all four corners join together the beams, posts and wall-plates and help stabilise the structure.

The beams in turn support the rafters which carry the roof covering. The low outer walls are not load-bearing but merely seal the structure.

The internal arrangement of the building is similar to that found in other hall-houses in the museum. Beyond the large portal is the threshing floor, with its clean sandstone flagstones which is flanked on either side by stalls and stables. The nesting boxes attached to the wall posts on the left indicate that hens were also kept in this area.

There is no dividing wall between the "farm" end of the building and the kitchen-cum-living area where most of the domestic work was done and where meals were taken.

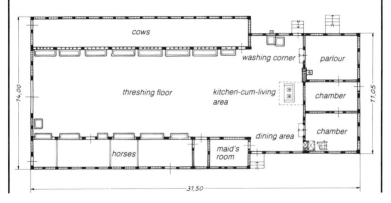

The interior of the farmhouse viewed from the entrance to the threshing floor, with cattle stalls to the left and stables to the right

The fireplace, complete with spark deflector, and the washing corner

To the left of the low stone fireplace, which does not have a chimney, is a chest containing salt, and on top of it stands a box which held the daily supply. Such a large quantity of salt was essential for preservation purposes. Within handy reach of the hearth are all the utensils necessary for cooking and tending the fire, such as a blow tube, a tripod, a coffee roaster (up on the fire-hood) and a number of other implements, most of them made of iron.

The bay frame immediately in front of the hearth is modified to allow for more working space or dwelling place for people. It has had the aisle post on the right withdrawn but you can still see the keyholes where it sat prior to the alteration. The open washing corner was lower from the beginning. The right hand alteration allowed for a higher wall and more light from larger windows.

At meal times the master of the house would sit at the head of the large dining table. Behind him, within easy reach, was the bread cupboard so that the farmer could distribute the bread. When the house was altered around 1600, a suite of rooms comprising a heated parlour and two chambers was added at the rear. The servants' quarters, which are next to the stables, were established at the same time.

The chamber on the right with its brightly painted four-poster bed and late-Gothic linen chest was the master bedroom. From here a flight of steps leads up to the loft, which was not only used for storing corn, but also served as additional sleeping space for either the servants or the children.

The parlour in the farmhouse

During the cold winter months the parlour which received its heat from the kitchen, was undoubtedly the only really warm room in the entire house. Its fixtures and fittings are those of the late 18th century. In more recent times the cast-iron stove, made in 1661, was used for baking a flat round cake made of grated potatoes and flour and known as *"pickert"*. The brightly coloured panelling comes from a farm in Linderhofe in the region of Lippe and gives the room a thoroughly contemporary feel. There is a picture on the wall to the right of the door which, depending on whether it is viewed from the front, the right or the left, displays one of three portraits of leading Protestants: Gustav Adolf of Sweden, Martin Luther and Philipp Melanchthon.

Between the parlour and the master bedroom lies another chamber which served either as a children's bedroom or as a store for linen. In the event of a fire, it was possible to escape though a "back door". The door near the wash-place opens on to the well, the mouth of which is shielded by a roof. To the right of the door there is a flight of steps leading down to the cellar which, in view of the size of the household (about 15 people altogether), must have been indispensible for storing items of food such as "sauerkraut" and cured meats.

T 2 Granary

from the Runksmeier-Krüger farm
in Kalletal-Brosen in the district of Lippe,
built around 1580,
dismantled in 1971 and re-erected in 1972 – 73

Like the farmhouse, which was built in the same year, this grain store provides further evidence of the fact that succeeding generations of timber-framed buildings in the Lippe region preserved all the qualities and techniques from the golden age of craftsmanship in the late Middle Ages. Nowhere is this more striking than in the powerful timbers that were used for the arch braces — the mark of an exceptionally sturdy and robust structure. Similarly, the joists in the ground floor ceiling are not only mortised to the wall posts but also appear in the spaces between them. This method of constructing buildings of more than one storey is typical of the late Middle Ages.

View of the rear gable of the Brosen granary

However, we must not overlook the aesthetic side of these lavishly built wood structures: The highly decorative profiles of the imposing and often curved timbers are a reflection of the importance attached to the cereals and seed-corn which this building contained. The richly carved brackets which support the overhanging gable reinforce this impression. The broad jettied roof helps keep the foundations and ground sills dry and sound.

T 3 Barn

from the Meier zu Bexten farm
in Bad Salzuflen-Wülfer-Bexten
in the district of Lippe,
built in 1599,
dismantled in 1971 and re-erected in 1972 – 73

At the time of construction, this double-aisled barn would have been exceptionally large for a building of its kind. It owes its size primarily to the fact that it came originally from the important Meier zu Bexten Farm where, as well as being a store for harvested crops, it served as a shelter for the sheep during the cold winter months. The small chamber beyond the door on the right in the front gable provided very spartan accommodation for the shepherd.

The exterior of the barn (the inscription above the door tells us that it was built in 1599) is as modest in appearance as the farmhouse. The curved braces which adorn the side walls are a simple but effective form of decoration which typify 16th century buildings in the Lippe region, as do the carved brackets that support the jettied front gables of this building, the granary and the farmhouse.

As it is a through-passage barn, there is another large door in the rear gable. The cart standing at the front of the building served as make-shift accommodation for the shepherd when out in the fields.

T 4 Dower house

from the Böltke farm,
in Detmold-Oettern-Bremke
in the district of Lippe,
built in 1619;
dismantled in 1969 and re-erected in 1972 – 73

This small building was where the farmer and his wife lived when they retired, having handed the farm on to their progeny. As the floor plan shows, the house is almost perfectly square. Because the working area was comparatively small, it was possible for the parlour, the chambers and the weaving room, and even the fireplace to be located in the side aisles. This arrangement produced a through-passage with a door at the rear which gave on to a small garden. The house contains all

The dower house: view of the threshing floor and garden from the main door

159

the prerequisites of a self-sufficient existence, albeit on a very modest scale. If finances allowed, a maid or farm-hand might have been employed, assuming of course that there were cattle to be tended. Indeed, the stalls provided accommodation for up to 3 cows. If the elderly members of the family were no longer alive, a building such as this would probably have been rented either to an artisan or a farmlabourer (see: "Cottages"). The names of the original owner and the builder are engraved above the door:

IOHAN. BÔLKE IN DER $\overline{\text{BREK}}$ MES. TER./
VAN. GIBEN. HAVE   HENRICK THOBEN
THO FROME.SEN   TERUP ANNO. 16.19

T 5 Bakehouse

from the Brede farm
in Detmold-Dehlentrup in the district of Lippe,
built in 1790,
dismantled in 1966 and re-erected in 1971 – 72

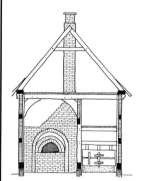
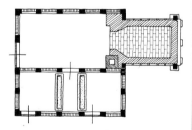

Cross-section and floor plan of the bakehouse, showing the oven, the chimney and the pigsty

In addition to a baking room, this building, which is the smallest on the farm, also contained two pigsties. This rather peculiar combination is explained by the fact that there were long intervals between baking days. Pantile roofs like the ones covering the two youngest buildings on the farm first appeared in the Lippe region in the late 18th century. As was customary, the vaulted oven is located outside the bakehouse where it stands on a wooden base and is protected by a pantile roof.

This particular oven is unusual in having a chimney to take away the smoke. The kneading trough has been fashioned from the trunk of an oak tree. Above the door, and bounded by the coats of arms of the Grafen v. Sternberg (the rose of Lippe and a star), is an inscription plaque, which became a characteristic form of decoration on farmhouses in this region from the late 17th century.

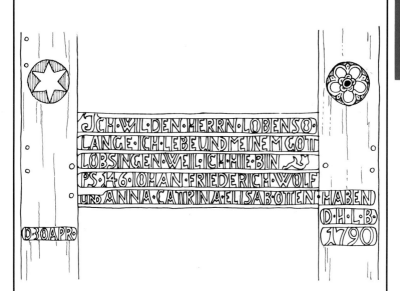

T 6 Multi-purpose granary

from the Obermeier farm
in Blomberg-Brüntrup in the district of Lippe,
built in 1790,
dismantled in 1969 and re-erected in 1971 – 72

In common with many of the slightly younger buildings to be found in the Lippe region, the timbers of this two-storey multi-purpose granary are comparatively slender. The symmetrical arrangement of the curved braces in all four outer walls is a particularly striking decorative feature. Down the left-hand side of the building, where hens are now kept, there used to be a pigsty and a wood store. All manner of bee-keeping equipment can be seen in the room on the right. Here too the door frame is embossed with finely carved inscriptions:

161

Inscription left-hand door

Right-hand door:

> IOHANN HENRICH.BOHMER
> AUS DER VOGELHORST
> UND.SOPHIA.ELEONO
> RA.MEIERS.VON ISTRUP
>
> D. 29 TEN   ANNO
> IULIUS   1790

T 7 Apiary

Klashörster farm,
Verl, district of Gütersloh,
built around 1800;
dismantled and re-erected in 1985

Apiaries are located at a short distance from the farms so that the bees can swarm out into the gardens and fields. The hives must not be exposed to direct sunlight and must be placed in a way to avoid the flying direction of the bees crossing the farmyard and streets where most people have to walk.

The post and beam structure of the half timbered house, built around 1800, has narrow openings at the back and lateral fronts, consisting of four or six posts, respectively, forming chains of nogging beams. All openings are infilled with brick. The front shows a different pattern. The posts are arranged further apart and are connected by six beams in a tight sequence (six on top of each other), providing sufficient space for the beehives which can be placed one above the other. The narrow structure secures the beehives against theft.
The small size of the building (4.45×2.10) allowed transportation of the apiary from Verl to Detmold in one piece without any dismantling or infilling.

X 1 Bell tower

from Rödinghausen-Schwenningdorf
in the district of Herford,
built in 1877,
dismantled in 1966 and re-erected in 1978

In many rural areas where the farms were often several miles from each other
and from the church, bell towers were erected at suitable intervals. The peal of
the bell would announce such events as deaths, marriages and fires.

As one of the inscriptions on the bell confirms,

1877 ANGESCHAFFT DURCH DIE INTERESSENTEN DER GEHÖFTE V. D. DRIFT,

it was commissioned and paid for by the inhabitants of the outlying farms in the parish of Schwenningdorf. It is made of cast-
steel from Bochum and bears the monogram **B. V. G.** It was
dedicated to Martin Luther, whose name appears on the back.
The honorary office of bell-ringer rotated annually, and the bell
was still being rung in 1966 by one of the neighbouring farmers
in return for an annual honorarium of 50 Pfennigs.

Bell tower in front of the farmhouse of the Minden farm

The boundary between Rekkenberg and Rietberg was redrawn in 1774. The province of Reckenberg, which was governed from Wiedenbrück, was once an exclave of the prince-bishopric of Osnabrück. In 1803 it came under the jurisdiction of Hannover and was eventually ceded to Prussia in 1815. The county of Rietberg remained politically autonomous until 1807, but it too fell to Prussia in 1815. A wheel with six spokes, which was the emblem of the prince-bishopric of Osnabrück, is engraved on one face of the stone, whilst the other side displays an eagle, representing the county of Rietberg.

X 2 Boundary stone

from the district of Gütersloh, implanted after 1774; transplanted in 1977

This tall, slender boundary stone, on which the markings made by the mason's chisel are still clearly visible, denotes the border between the principality of Lippe and the Prussian province of Westphalia (formerly the princedom of Paderborn). On one side is the rose of Lippe with its five petals and the number 24 D (boundary stones were numbered consecutively) and on the other the Prussian eagle and the date 1860.

X 3 Boundary stone

from Senne on the border between
the districts of Lippe and Paderborn,
implanted in 1860 and transplanted in 1977

The quarry-stone bridge of Horn prior to being dismantled 1979 and after its re-erection

X 4 Bridge

from Holzhauser Berg in Horn
in the district of Lippe,
built in 1876,
dismantled in 1979 and re-erected in 1980 – 81

In 1979 the bridge over the Wiembecke at the edge of the town of Horn on the road to Holzhauser Berg had to make way for a road-widenening scheme. At the head of each arch ist a commemorative keystone, one of which carries the year 1876 (above it is another stone bearing the coat of arms of the town of Horn), whilst the other displays an anchor.

Y 1 – 4 Service buildings

Y 1 Main restaurant

(planned)

Y 2 Restaurant

formerly Kiencker-Niederhellmann house
from Lienen in the district of Steinfurt,
built in 1756;
dismantled in 1963 and re-erected in 1971 – 72

This small artisan's house comes from Lienen where the streets were narrow and cramped, which explains why the side walls are very tall when compared with those of a detached cottage. Most of the doors and windows have been replaced by ones which are more in keeping with its new role in the Museum. However, the original entrance door, which is much more lavishly constructed than most, has been retained. The joists between the individual wings are underlined by a framework of strong decorative posts. The layout of the interior remains virtually unaltered: Beyond the threshing floor was the kitchen, and two small chambers adjoined the stalls on the right. The door-surround is decorated with artisans' symbols, and the inscription on the lintel reads:

Es müssen alle meine Feinde zu schanden werden und sehr
erschrecken PS. 6 vs. 11
C. H. Kiencker   A. Agn. Metgers
Anno 1756   Den 6ten Juli
M/P · B

The house is now a small cafeteria called the "Tiergartenkrug". This name was chosen because it is situated in a part of the Museum which the princes of Lippe turned into an animal park. Sections of the wall with which it was enclosed can still be seen nearby.

Y 3 Public convenience

formerly a pigsty attached to Beelen parsonage,
Beelen, in the district of Warendorf,
built in the 18th century
dismantled in 1966 and re-erected in 1971

Although the interior of this building has been altered to accommodate its new use, the exterior remains faithful to its 18th century origins.

Y 4 Public convenience

formerly a stable on the Wintrup Estate
in Steinheim-Wintrup in the district of Höxter,
built in the 18th century;
dismantled and re-erected in 1981

The public convenience in the Paderborn Village was once the stable on the Wolff-Metternich Estate in Wintrup near Vinsebeck. It was built of quarry-stone in the 18th century and, according to the inscription on the lintel, was extended in 1827. This lintel obviously came from another building, because the date 1803 is engraved on its underside. Indeed, the stable is comprised to a large extent of the remains of a much grander Renaissance building, and this includes the stones inlaid with strapwork and the mask of a lion (which was perhaps originally part of a portal), as well as the roof timbers, which were first employed as long ago as 1593.

The Kiencker-Niederhellmann house and pigsty from Beelen, which is now the cafeteria

Z 1 – 5　Administration and operational buildings

Z 1 – 3　Entrance complex (including exhibition hall and administrative buildings)

(planned)

Z 4　Construction unit

built in 1974;
comprises the joining and trimming hall,
the restoration workshops,
garages and several
facilities for the craftsmen

Z 5　Horticultural unit

Dower house, Grote farm,
Detmold-Spork-Eichholz, district of Lippe,
built in 1763;
dismantled in 1960, re-erected in 1987 – 88

The small four post and beam house with its exceptionally narrow structural arrangement of 60 cubic meters of oakwood accommodates the gardener's of the open air museum. This is where the cultivation of the historical gardens is prepared, and from where the entire parks and gardens are maintained. Apart from many species of plants, the ancient species of domestic animals are accommodated during the winter.

Drawings and photographs by:

K. H. Baumeister, Dortmund: 79

Becker, Beckum: 132

H. Fender, Osnabrück: 131

H. G. Gessner, Bielefeld: 67, 71, 89 b, 90 b, 96 b, 104, 108, 120, 138 b, 140 b, 145, 146, 154 b, 155, 157

B. Dahlhoff, Eickelborn: 85

Hamburger-Aero-Lloyd: 149

W. Hansen, Detmold: 160

Holtmann, Münster: 143

K. Klöckner, Hanau: 96 a

H. Kreft, Minden: 144 b, 154 a

Landesbildstelle Westfalen, Münster: 84, 109 b

Lippisches Landesmuseum, Detmold: 117

L. Nolte, Amelunxen: 35

Ochsenfarth, Paderborn: 40, 62 a

H. von Rouppert, Wiedenbrück: 42

G. Rudolf, Neue Westfälische, Bielefeld: 106, 107

J. Schepers, Münster: 78 b

Seiger, Sennestadt: 21, 25, 87, 93, 97, 105, 109 a, 118, 164 a, 164 b, 165 a, 165 b

B. Socha, Münster: 17, 91, 110, 122, 126, 127, 136 b, 137, 148, 162

A. Starke, Detmold: 113

F. Walter, Münster: 88

E. Schlingmann/Westfälisches Freilichtmuseum, Detmold (Lehmann, Potthoff): 16, 19, 26, 28 b, 33 b, 43 b, 47, 54, 68, 78 a, 81, 89 a, 102, 121 a, 136 a, 140 a, 144 a, 152, 153 b, 159 b

D. Werschbizkij, Münster: 65, 76, 86, 100, 119, 134, 142, 151 a

Westfälisches Amt für Baupflege, Münster: 115

Westfälisches Amt für Denkmalpflege (Vössing), Münster: 41

Westfälisches Freilichtmuseum, Detmold: 52, 57, 112 a, 112 b, 129

Baumeier 60, 166 a; Droege 13, 28 a, 33 a, 43 a, 90 a, 99, 163; Großmann 10, 11, 13, 14, 15, 18, 27, 29, 31, 37, 39, 45, 62 b, 62 c, 64, 75, 82, 116, 136 b; Hehre 130; Kelle 59, 69, 83, 98, 124 b, 151 b; Könenkamp 159 a; Lüttmann 22; Obertopp 92, 94 b; Potthoff 28 b, 44, 54, 72, 73, 77, 81, 94 a, 114, 124 a, 128, 161; Schepers 20, 101, 121 b, 135, 138 a, 141 a, 141 b; Sternschulte 50; Watermann 139

Jacket photograph by H. G. Gessner, Design by H. Wasgindt

Map of Westphalia and museum: H. Wasgindt

Publications of the Westphalian Open Air Museum

Published by order of Landschaftsverband Westfalen-Lippe (regional federation)
by Stefan Baumeier

Series: Papers

Volume 1: Josef Schepers, Der Lippische Meierhof
Volume 2: Kurt Dröge, Spanschachteln, Bestandskatalog
Volume 3: G. Ulrich Großmann und Ingrid Schulte, Die Bockwindmühle
Volume 4: Kurt Dröge unter Mitarbeit von Regina Fritsch und Anita Switalski, Sprüche zur Konfirmation — Bilder zur Erstkommunion
Volume 5: Christoph Gerlach, Fenster aus Westfalen
Volume 6: Ernst H. Segschneider unter Mitarbeit von Martin Westphal, Zeichen der Not

Series: Guides

Guide 1: Ingrid Schulte/G. Ulrich Großmann, Die Kappenwindmühle
Guide 2: Helmut Sydow/G. Ulrich Großmann, Die Bockwindmühle
Guide 3: Kurt Dröge, Die Schule aus Thöningsen
Guide 4: Ernst Helmut Segschneider, Die Töpferei
Guide 5: Agnes Sternschulte, Die Gärten
Guide 6: Regina Fritsch, Das Brigittenhäuschen
Guide 7: Stefan Baumeier/Marianne Jacoby-Zakfeld, Das Stahlsche Haus
Guide 8: Katharina Schlimmgen-Ehmke: Die Leibzucht aus Rischenau
Guide 9: Joachim Kleinmanns: Die Spritzenhäuser

Series: Contributions to Folklore and House Research

Published by Stefan Baumeier
and Kurt Dröge,
Volume 1/1986
Volume 2/1987
Volume 3/1988

		Designation of building	Place of origin	Date of construction
①	A 5	Church Yard Granary	Borchen-Etteln	1576
②	A 6	Church Yard Granary	Anröchte-Mellrich	1505
③	A 9	Farmhouse Valepage farm	Delbrück-Dorfbauerschaft	1577, 19th cnt
④	A 10	Multi purpose barn	Warstein-Westendorf	1763
⑤	A 11	Granary	Salzkotten-Winkhausen	1561
⑥	A 12	Fruit drying kiln	Höxter-Falkenflucht	19th cnt
⑦	A 13	Tenanted cottage Dower house	Lügde-Rischenau	1732/1830
⑧	A 14	Farmhouse	Emmerthal-Grohnde	1731
⑨	A 15	Barn	Emmerthal-Kirchohsen	1624/30
⑩	A 17	Well	Schieder-Schwalenberg	12th cnt
		Well	Höxter-Godelheim	19th cnt
⑪	A 18	Smithy	Höxter-Godelheim	1777
⑫	A 19	Wayside chapel	Rietberg-Westerwiehe	1697
⑬	A 20	Moven house	Höxter-Bruchhausen	1651
⑭	A 21	Golücke house	Beverungen-Amelunxen	1767
⑮	A 22	Cowshed and lavatory	Höxter-Stahle	before 1830
⑯	A 23	Commerical bakehouse	Höxter-Stahle	1808
⑰	A 24	Schönhof	Wiedenbrück	around 1720
⑱	A 25	Fire station	Schlangen-Kohlstädt	1835
⑲	A 26	Summerhouse	Höxter-Godelheim	18th cnt 1842/46
⑳	A 28	The Stahl House	Gütersloh	1730
㉑	A 29	Brigitte house	Rietberg	1602, 19th cnt
㉒	A 31	Farmhouse	Emmerthal-Grohnde	1622/1909
㉓	A 34	Ludovici house	Bad Driburg-Neuenheerse	1608/14, 1777
㉔	A 59	Craftsman's house	Blomberg	1450, 1610

For number in circle re. map of Westphalia inside the front jacket.

		Designation of building	Place of origin	Date of construction
㉕	A 60	Town farmer's house	Holzminden	1677
㉖	A 61	Fire station	Lügde-Hummersen	1839
㉗	A 80	Chapel	Delbrück-Westenholz	1775
㉘	C 1	Farmhouse	Finnentrop-Ostentrop	1770
㉙	E 1	Tower mill	Rahden-Tonnenheide	1789, 1842
㉚	E 2	Barn	Herten	1695
㉛	E 4	Post mill	Groß-Lobke	1812
㉜	E 6	Water mill	Melle-Barkhausen	1731/1841
㉝	H 1	Farmhouse	Dortmund-Brackel	1793
㉞	H 2	Gatehouse	Dortmund-Eichlinghofen	around 1704
㉟	H 4	Granary	Olfen-Vinnum	1727
㊱	H 5	Fire station	Welver-Einecke	1846
㊲	H 6	School	Soest-Thöningsen	1837
㊳	H 7	Apiary	Dortmund-Eichlinghofen	1880/81
㊴	J 1	Farmhouse	Borken-Rhedebrügge	1789 – 90
㊵	J 2	Barn	Vreden-Ellewick	around 1775
㊶	J 3	Shed	Schöppingen-Tinge	1743
㊷	J 4	Bakehouse	Gescher-Büren	1747
㊸	J 5	Clay coated granary	Neuenhaus-Grasdorf	1454
㊹	J 7	Corn granary	Havixbeck-Lasbeck	around 1820
㊺	J 8	Oat barn	Velen-Holthausen	19th cnt
㊻	J 9	Flax oven	Stadtlohn-Hengeler	around 1860
㊼	J 10	Hay barn	Bentfeld	around 1900
㊽	K 1	Farmhouse	Albersloh-Alst	1787
㊾	K 2	Gatehouse	Münster-Nienberge	1767
㊿	K 3	Wood shed	Harsewinkel-Beller	around 1860

For number in circle re. map of Westphalia inside the front jacket.

			Designation of building	Place of origin	Date of construction
(51)	K	4	New granary	Harsewinkel-Beller	1711
(52)	K	5	Bakehouse	Harsewinkel-Beller	1695
(53)	K	6	Old granary	Everswinkel-Wieningen	1565
(54)	K	7	Bleaching hut	Everswinkel-Schuter	around 1860
(55)	K	9	Through passage barn	Senden-Schölling	1796
(56)	K	10	Pigsty	Greven	17th cnt
(57)	K	11	Lavatory	Reconstruction	acc. to 19th century
(58)	K	12	Sheepfold	Wettringen-Dorfbauerschaft	around 1700
(59)	L	1	Krummes Haus (crooked house)	Detmold	around 1680
(60)	L	2	Pheasantry	Detmold	1836–38
(61)	O	1	Farmhouse	Bramsche-Kalkriese	1609
(62)	O	2	Sheepfold	Bramsche-Kalkriese	1792
(63)	O	3	Barn	Bissendorf-Holte-Sünsbeck	1763
(64)	O	4	Pigsty	Bramsche-Schleptrup	1827
(65)	O	5	Bakehouse granary	Ostercappeln-Schwagstorf	1710, 1810
(66)	O	6	Apiary	Warmsen-Hauskämpen	around 1860
(67)	O	7	Bleaching hut	Gersten	around 1840
(68)	O	8	Lavatory	Reconstruction	acc. to 19th cnt
(69)	O	9	Pottery	Hagen-Gellenbeck	1828
(70)	P	1	Tecklenburg Kotten	Mettingen-Höveringhausen	1784
(71)	P	2	Doppelheuerhaus	Bad Essen-Hüsede	1609/1738
(72)	Q	1	Farmhouse	Raddestorf-Kleinenheerse	1673
(73)	Q	2	Granary	Rahden	1712

For number in circle re. map of Westphalia inside the front jacket.

			Designation of building	Place of origin	Date of construction
(74)	Q	3	Pigsty	Petershagen-Buchholz	around 1585
(75)	Q	4	Woodshed	Rahden-Wehe	around 1625
(76)	Q	5	Bakehouse	Espelkamp-Frotheim	1614
(77)	Q	6	Barn	Warmsen-Bohnhorst	1671
(78)	Q	7	Fire barn	Diepenau-Nordel	around 1700
(79)	Q	8	Lavatory	Reconstruction	acc. to 17th century
(80)	T	1	Farmhouse	Lemgo-Leese	1570
(81)	T	2	Granary	Kalletal-Brosen	around 1580
(82)	T	3	Barn	Bad Salzuflen-Wülfer-Bexten	1599
(83)	T	4	Dower house	Detmold-Oettern-Bremke	1619
(84)	T	5	Bakehouse	Detmold-Dehlentrup	1790
(85)	T	6	Multi-purpose granary	Blomberg-Brüntrup	1790
(86)	T	7	Apiary	Verl	around 1800
	X	1	Bell tower	Rödinghausen-Schwenningdorf	1877
	X	2	Boundary stone	(district of Gütersloh)	after 1744
	X	3	Boundary stone	(Senne)	1860
	X	4	Bridge	Horn	1876
(87)	Y	2	Restaurant	Lienen	1756
(88)	Y	3	Public convenience/ Pigsty	Beelen	18th cnt
(89)	Y	4	Public convenience/ stable	Steinheim-Wintrup	18th century, 1827
(90)	Z	5	Gardener's/Dower house	Detmold-Spork-Eichholz	1763

General Information for Visitors to the Museum

Funding authority: Landschaftsverband Westfalen-Lippe
Museum Director: Dr. Stefan Baumeier

Opening times: 1 April to 31 October
Daily from 9.00 to 18.00 (no admission after 17.00). Closed on Mondays (unless Monday is a public holiday)

Educational Packs are available to schools (postage not possible) and teachers' material can be supplied on receipt of payment.
Guided tours must be booked in writing and paid for in advance.
Vehicle park and **bus stop** off the district road between the centre of Detmold and Detmold-Heiligenkirchen.
Changing Exhibitions in the barn from Westendorf (A 10).

Museum Shop (Prints, postcards, posters, products of the museum) in the house from Grohnde (A 14) Paderborn village.

Rest areas of the West Hellweg Farm, Osnabrück Farm (under cover), the meadow on the Minden Farm, meadow by the Tower Mill, the Sheepfold on the moated farm.

Restaurant "Tiergartenkrug" next to the moated "Gräftenhof" farm (Y 2), Tel. (0 52 31) 2 71 61
Restaurant "Zum Wilden Mann" in the house from Grohnde (A 14), the Paderborn Village, Tel. (0 52 31) 2 16 30
Opening times are the same as those for the Museum.
Leased by: Landesverband Lippe,
Schloß Brake, 4920 Lemgo
Tel. (0 52 61) 25 02-0

WC by the Tiergartenkrug (Y 3)
WC in the Paderborn Village (Y 4)

Smoking is not permitted in the Museum buildings.
Dogs must be kept on a lead.
The taking of **photographs** is permitted, but not for commercial purposes.
Enquiries: Westfälisches Freilichtmuseum, Krummes Haus, D-4930 Detmold, Tel. (0 52 31) 706-0
Telefax (0 52 31) 7 06-1 06